# Behind Their Brand: Chef Edition Vol. 2

## Compiled by Deb Cantrell

## Co-authored by:

Deb Miley

Tracey Callahan

Walda Collins

Alicia Ojeda

Donna Barrow

Elizabeth Bourget

Gina VanderKooi

Jodi Giroux

Shirley Scrafford

Behind Their Brand: Chef Edition, Vol. 2

Behind Their Brand: Chef Edition, Vol. 2

1. Business 2. Internet
ISBN-10: 1537751158
ISBN-13: 978-1537751153
Development / Business Development

# TABLE OF CONTENTS

# Introduction

When you think of chefs a certain image probably comes to mind. Perhaps you imagine a chef wearing a tall, white hat working in a five-star restaurant, garnishing a fancy dish.

While there are many chefs like that, there are also non-traditional chefs who are little different from the rest of the pack. These non-traditional chefs are those who have ventured outside other's expectations for them as chefs and have forged their own path of owning a culinary business, whether that be a catering company, a personal chef business or being a private chef cooking in someone's home.

I have been in the culinary industry for over 15 years and have owned a variety of culinary businesses including a restaurant, catering company and now my personal chef company, Savor Culinary Services and my coaching company, Chef Deb. I think it's safe to say I know a thing or two about how much work goes into owning a business. With the help of amazing mentors and learning through trial and error, I have been able to build successful businesses.

Several years ago I realized that I wanted to help other chefs grow their culinary business and avoid mistakes I had made and get the guidance they deserve in a field where there aren't many formal culinary business coaches.

I wanted to compile a book that featured chefs with all different professional backgrounds, tastes and different culinary businesses who have a story to share. Each of the chefs featured in this book I have had the honor of working with personally. We have shared long phone calls, we have cried together, celebrated victories together, and have even flown across the country to brainstorm and solve problems together.

I wish I could take all the credit for their success, but it has been their hard work and perseverance that has led them to building a successful brand. Their dedication has been so inspiring to me and I amazed each day with their unrelenting entrepreneurial spirits.

As you turn the pages of this book and read each of their stories, I hope you will be inspired to follow your dreams and not be afraid to be "less conventional" in your field.

Mentoring these chefs has certainly showed me that good things come to those who work hard, are humble and are willing to step out of their comfort zone and take risks.

I wish you success wherever your dreams take you!

Deb Cantrell
Founder, Savor Culinary Services
Compiler, Behind Their Brand: Chef Edition Vol 1 & 2

# CHEF DEB MILEY
## Founder, Deb Miley Dishes

**Share with us what your business is and why you wanted to start this business.**

Deb Miley Dishes is the culmination of my unadulterated love for food and cooking, bringing simply good food to your family's table so that you can enjoy life's simplest moments and greatest milestones together — all with an amazing meal at the heart of it.

I'm a self-taught home cook, and I've spent the last 20 years exploring and perfecting my craft. My skills have been enhanced over the last decade as my family crisscrossed the country and world. From New York to California and now Chicago, I have broadened my classic Italian and American menus with Midwestern and West Coast flair. A one-year residence in Paris with my husband, Greg, and two children, Olivia and Tripp, offered me the opportunity to take advantage of all French cooking has to offer, infusing my style with local classics and traditional European flavors. Having lived all across the US and in Paris, I have a deep appreciation for full flavors and native cooking techniques, all of which have brought to life my desire to share delicious food with my clients.

**What was your motivation for becoming a chef and/or starting your own business?**

I was inspired to start Deb Miley Dishes because I know firsthand how challenging a busy schedule and limited time can be when you are trying to shop for and prepare home-cooked meals. I also know that there's nothing better than a freshly-cooked meal awaiting you at the end of a long day. I often say there's an Italian grandmother trapped inside my body! Not unlike the best Nonnas I know, I just want to feed people, and there's always something brewing in my kitchen.

My story started in the 1970's, growing up in a deeply-rooted Italian immigrant neighborhood in Brooklyn, New York. On most days, you could walk down any block and smell fresh basil, sauce simmering on the stove, or sausage being cooked. There were fresh pasta stores, butchers, salumerias, fruit markets, and pizzerias. Every kind of Italian food you could imagine was within a few blocks of home, or even closer — at our neighbors' houses. As a young teenager, I started working at a neighborhood salumeria, and as I watched them make fresh mozzarella and loaves of bread, I was inspired by all the flavors the Italian food culture had to offer.

At the same time, my mother — the first generation American daughter of Irish immigrants, and a great cook — always encouraged my curiosity and allowed me the freedom to explore in the kitchen. She and my grandmother, Ita Molloy, who came to the US as a teenager with the hopes of living the American dream, influenced my love for traditional, Irish-American comfort food with all the trimmings. It was in my mother's kitchen that I learned to master a proper roux, roast beef with mashed potatoes and scratch-made gravy, and the all-American Thanksgiving table we all look forward to every November. I continue to fully stock my pantry year-round with Bell's Seasoning, my grandmother's secret ingredient for stuffing. Between the Irish-American traditional comforts passed down from my family and the rich influence of our Italian friends and family, I was immersed in many different tastes and cultures. I didn't know it at the time, but all of these experiences would one day lay the foundation for my business.

I later found myself working very long hours in a job that I loved while living at home with my parents in Brooklyn. I remember calling them up during the day, asking them want they wanted for dinner, then going home to cook for the three of us. It was just a way for me to unwind and relax, but during those nights, I learned that the kitchen was the place I felt most confident, energized, and excited.

As I kept practicing and learning, as well as taking some recreational cooking classes, the idea of changing careers and becoming a chef was something that I started to seriously consider.

The primary goal for my business — beyond ensuring that the food was great — was to make sure it felt personal and unique, just like cooking for someone at home. I wanted my clients to feel as though I was giving them a part of myself and connecting with them on a very intimate level.

The nights in my parents' kitchen started me on my journey toward becoming a chef, and from the time my kids were babies, I passed on to them my love for food and my curiosity in the kitchen. Our travels enhanced my delight in food cultures and flavors and broadened my senses and creativity. In 2013, I purchased the domain name "Deb Miley Dishes" and decided that I would wait for the right time to become an entrepreneur. Though I didn't know precisely what my business would look like or what I would offer, I was confident that the time was right to start preparing for its launch.

**What have you learned about yourself through running your business?**

First and foremost, as personal as this business is, it's still a business; not everyone will enjoy or appreciate what I have to offer. Tastes, palates, and needs are different; this is an extremely tough lesson for a people-pleaser like me to learn. I try to remember something I heard on this topic that really resonates with me: "You can be the sweetest, juiciest peach in the world, but there are just some people who don't like peaches." I stay focused on being authentic, and I believe that will help me connect with the right clients and evolve my skills and business.

Another valuable lesson I've learned: hire people who are experts to do what you are not equipped to do. I excel at "getting sh*t done," or GSD, as I like to call it. I'm proficient in growing a marriage and family, running a household, relocating homes and countries, managing youth travel hockey teams, and balancing the lives of two amazing kids, all while whipping something up on a moment's notice to feed anyone who is hungry! I'm extremely well-practiced in GSD. However, I'm not proficient in accounting, writing contracts, web and graphic design, label-making, analytics, and many other important things that are needed to run a successful business. I seek out and hire people who are qualified in these areas, believe in my business, and also bring a GSD approach to the table.

**What three things do you wish you would have known when you started?**

First, I think starting a new business is like having your first child; if you had actually known what you were going to experience, you probably never would've done it! But not unlike parenthood, starting a business can be one of the most exciting, challenging, rewarding, and hysterical experiences you can be blessed with!

Secondly, I wish I could've been absolutely certain of success. None of us wants to fail or hear the words "I knew you couldn't do it." Starting a business involves real risks — both financial and emotional — and it takes strength, courage, and fortitude. Success for me today is different than it was a year ago, and it will certainly be different two years from now.

Finally, I wish I had learned earlier on that you need to find the right execution support (my GSD approach referenced above). I learned this lesson the hard way about 15 years ago when I committed to doing a pro bono event for an acquaintance. It seemed easy breezy at the time. I was contemplating culinary school, and it was a great opportunity to figure out if this was the right career path for me. A simple-enough Bat Mitzvah brunch for a small group of people with a limited menu of kugels, bagels, lox, and some fruit platters — nothing I couldn't handle. Or so I thought!

I eagerly put the menu and my plan of action together, realizing I would need two people I could rely on to help me execute my plan on the day of the event. Two family members volunteered — both masters of GSD in their own lives — and we were off! It was a disaster — me, the event, everything! I relied on the help of two people who neither knew their way around the kitchen nor how to cook. While amazingly skilled in their respective professions, as well as successful and knowledgeable in many, many ways, I asked them to do something they didn't want to do, like to do, or know how to do. This didn't set us up for success. Lesson learned: hire the right people for the right job. I think we all may be over it now, but "bagel-gate" has never been discussed since!

**Can you share some early challenges in your business career and how you have learned to overcome them?**

Shifting from cooking as a hobby and personal passion to cooking as a profession was a tough transition for me. Cooking for people was an outlet and something that I enjoyed doing as a hobby. It was really challenging to place a monetary value on my cooking and my service. I was having a conversation with a dear friend of mine, a successful businesswoman in her own right, and she said, "Deb, this is not your hobby anymore." I realized then and there that I needed to change my mindset. When I did that, it was easier to embrace the value proposition of the business I'm in.

Another challenge that I needed to overcome was timing. There is never a "right time" to start your business. There will always be some obstacle, so you need to decide when you're going to make it happen. If you want to start a business, start today. Take one small step toward success and living your passion every day. Time is going to march on, so you may as well spend it doing something you love.

**What three characteristics describe what has made you successful and why?**

A good friend, who is a health and nutrition coach, believes that we should eat a rainbow of food every day to keep our bodies healthy. I agree with her, and I also believe that it takes a rainbow of different attributes and characteristics to achieve success in any business. The food industry specifically requires that you have a certain level of grit and tenacity, as well as an extremely thick skin, to survive and thrive in the kitchen. Growing up in Brooklyn helped with the grit and thick skin. Starting to work at 12 years old groomed my tenacious, GSD nature and approach to life that has helped shape my business. I am not above any task, and I am agile and forward-thinking in the kitchen.

I've always been a dreamer. Dreaming big sparks creativity and inspires resourcefulness, which is imperative to pleasing a client, trying to solve a culinary challenge, or just trying to get more creative as you stretch and evolve. As the song goes, "Dream on, dream until your dream comes true."

**How have you defined your voice in your market?**

I believe there's a place for everyone's culinary point of view, voice, and style; each chef I've met has something special to contribute. I'd like to think that I can bring a family back around their table with my food, or that I can help a client see a dream dinner come to life or experience an amazing meal as part of a special milestone. As I mentioned earlier, the primary goal for my business — beyond ensuring that the food is great — is to make sure it feels personal and unique, just like when I'm cooking for someone in my home.

I like to keep things authentic and simple, but I also haven't met a recipe that I didn't want to modify or amplify in some way. I love to look at recipes or menus and then work on how I can put my personal Deb Miley spin on them. When I lived in Paris, I often thought about Julia Child. As I walked the same markets she had walked more than 60 years prior, I realized that one of the most perfect things about Paris — for better or for worse — is that no matter how the world changes, there are certain things that will never change in Paris.

While living in France, I read Julia's book, *My Life in France,* and I often found myself laughing out loud at the similarity of the experiences we shared, although decades apart. But mostly, as I read her descriptive words about the different meats, foods, breads, and cheeses she explored, I found myself in parallel. I marveled at the very same cheeses, baguettes, sauces, foie gras, and wine. I felt a kinship with Julia.

The many lessons I learned in Paris helped me expand my own culinary point of view, which, in turn, demanded a higher level of creativity and food knowledge. But even more so, those lessons reminded me that, while I will always be growing and changing as a person, I need to remember to stay grounded to my roots and be true to who I am and the gifts I have to offer. My experiences and history make me unique as a person and a chef, and staying true to that history is what defines my voice and point of view.

**What would you advise someone who is struggling to build his or her brand?**

Be authentic. Figure out what makes your culinary point of view unique and stick to it. Talk it out with people you trust — within and outside of the business — so you can refine your "pitch" and reason for being.

Be consistent. Build a robust repository of assets that you can use persistently and consistently. While you may infuse new imagery to refresh your assets a few times a year, consistency will make your client feel a sense of stability and confidence in your brand. This will translate into trust.

Be social. From social media to traditional methods like referrals and in-person networking, keep talking with and meeting new people. Always be on the lookout for inspiration through interaction.

**Staying motivated when things don't seem to be coming together is a challenge at times. How do you motivate yourself? How would you advise someone else?**

Staying motivated is really hard, especially in the first year, when you're laying the foundation for your business, hiring experts and resources that you can't yet afford, and trying — often seemingly with little luck — to build a committed client base. I try to remind myself that this time is just like having a newborn. The sleepless nights eventually end, you find your rhythm, the fun part starts, and there is a bright light at the end of that dark, lonely, sleep-deprived tunnel. This newborn phase of building the business is critical, as it creates a strong foundation for you to continue to build upon as your business grows.

When I find myself needing some motivation, I think about the values Greg and I are trying to instill in our children:

- Work hard. Do your best. Don't give up. Don't let anyone tell you that you can't. This too shall pass.

We try to live those lessons in order to teach those values. And sometimes, I just think about those who may secretly want me to fail, and I say to myself, "Get up and get to it." Failure is not an option.

**One of the biggest struggles entrepreneurs have is how to price themselves. What advice would you share about pricing your services and offerings?**

Pricing was a struggle as I launched Deb Miley Dishes. I had to place a monetary value on my life's passion and charge people I knew for my services, all while being mindful of not undervaluing myself. Carefully considering the soft costs (menu planning, consultations, etc.) against the hard costs (sourcing products and the cooking itself) forced me to continuously assess my pricing structure to strike a balance of my costs against the perceived value of my services.

Eventually, I was able to demystify pricing by realizing that pricing for this type of business can be scalable and based primarily on logistics. If you run your business in a large, metropolitan city serving a clientele with a higher median income, your prices will scale to that income level. The same holds true if you live in a small, rural town.

It can be difficult for some clients to understand the value of a personal chef fee. They often don't realize the amount of effort, time, and creativity that goes into producing fresh menus, sourcing ingredients, and prepping and cooking food. There is also a whole level of back office administration that goes into running a successful business, and usually we pay accountants and graphic designers to help support that component.

I learned how important it is not to undervalue your product because it doesn't do anything to elevate your brand, your food, or your peer set. Part of being in an elite network of personal chefs and caterers is having the responsibility of elevating the profession and serving as ambassadors of the industry. When you elevate your business, your food, and your brand, you're elevating and supporting personal chefs everywhere.

**What advice would you give to a chef entrepreneur who is ready to take his or her business to the next level?**

My best advice for anyone who is in business or wants to take a business to the next level is to get a board of directors. Gather a group of people that you trust and can rely on for smart advice and honest feedback — good or bad. Their contribution is critical to shaping and driving your business. My board of directors is comprised of family and friends from different professional backgrounds. I go to them for advice about obstacles I'm facing, challenges that need solving, or thoughts on new pricing or programs. Like any good CEO, I process and consider their counsel to help make decisions. When all else fails, I go to my home base — my kids — for their insight. You'd be amazed at what sage advice tweens and teens have to offer. They ask perceptive, intuitive questions, can be (painfully) candid, and have practical, unadulterated perspectives on the world.

I also suggest that you find an expert coach or mentor. You can't be the chief cook and bottle washer and also be a business development guru. You need an expert that can fill that role for you, who can help you build a blueprint for growth and define the steps you need to get there. It will cost your business good money to hire the right person, but it's an investment that will allow you to grow your business while you GSD in the kitchen.

**What "must-have" resources would you recommend someone use in his or her business?**

When I decided to start Deb Miley Dishes, my first order of business was to create a website. I wanted the website to resonate with my customers and be authentic to who I am as a person, so I hired the right expert, and he did an amazing job. But I wish I had realized that my website is just a very small piece of my overall social media presence and is not static — it will be changing and growing as my business does.

In today's minute-by-minute selfie-posting, snapchatting world, a comprehensive social media presence is probably at the top of my list for a new business. With so much "noise" and information swirling around, consistent self-promotion of your business is critical. Find the right social media experts early in the process to help you create a comprehensive marketing and media strategy for your business. Maintaining a strong social media presence takes a lot of time and creativity, and hopefully you will be so busy in the kitchen that you will need to rely on an expert to help manage this for you.

Going back to my previous comments, I think it's imperative to gather a board of directors that you trust and can rely on for smart advice and honest feedback — good or bad. I rely on my BOD for all kinds of things — menus, photos, programs, pricing, mistakes I've made and how to fix them, generating more business, recipe-testing, and editing. (You all know who you are, and thank you from the bottom of my heart!) The bottom line is this: you don't know what you don't know. But there are people who have come before you who *do* know. Seek them out and rely on their experience. Then make dinner for them!

**What do you do for work life/balance and to take care of yourself?**

As an entrepreneur, my life is my work and my work is my life. It's all connected and messy. Some days it's fun and manageable, and other days I just can't wait to get home to my family. I love to be at home, in my kitchen, hearing about everyone's day and making a meal for my family. I'm so blessed to have an amazing husband, kids, and extended family who unconditionally love and support me, as well as some spectacular girlfriends who are always there to listen to my latest adventures. And when all else fails, shopping and wine do the trick!

# Continue the Conversation with Chef Deb Miley:

Deb Miley Dishes brings simply good food to your family's table, so you can enjoy life's simplest moments or greatest milestones together - all with an amazing meal at the heart of it. I'm a self-taught home cook who has spent the last 20 years exploring and perfecting my craft. My skills have been enhanced over the last decade as my family crisscrossed the country and world. From New York to California and now Chicago, I have broadened my classic Italian and American menus with Mid-Western and West Coast flair.

A 1-year residence in Paris with my husband, Greg, and two children, Olivia and Tripp, offered me the opportunity to take advantage of all French cooking has to offer, infusing my style with local classics and traditional European flavors. Having lived all across the US and in Paris, I have a deep appreciation for full flavors and native cooking techniques, all of which has brought to life my desire to share delicious food with my clients.

I currently reside in the northern suburbs of Chicago with my ever-hungry husband and kids.

**Website:**
www.debmileydishes.com

# CHEF TRACEY CALLAHAN
## Founder, The Good Helper

**Share with us what your business is and why you wanted to start this business.**

Tracey Callahan is a classically trained chef from the Culinary Institute of America. Her love for cooking began as a child in the south end of Hartford, Connecticut's "Little Italy" and continued during her 23-year career in the US Air Force. While traveling across the globe, she gained an appreciation for local cuisines. She has tied her passion for food, travel, and helping others by sharing authentic cuisine with her clients, family, and friends.

In August 2010, she was recognized for her talents by winning a competition similar to "Iron Chef" while onboard the inaugural Celebrity Cruise Line/Food Network Eastern Caribbean cruise. Chefs Cat Cora and Aaron Sanchez were two of the judges for the event. It was the opportunity of a lifetime.

Tracey has a B.S. in Business Management from National Louis University, an A.S. in Culinary Arts from the Culinary Institute of America, and an A.S. in Communications Technology from the Community College of the Air Force. She is also a graduate of the Culinary Business Academy and is a member of the United States Personal Chef Association and Women Chefs and Restaurateurs.

Bonaiuto's, The Good Helper, Your Personal Chef, LLC provides personal chef services and culinary consulting services to a variety of clients. A personal chef is one who cooks for clients in the clients' homes, whether for weekly meals, dinner parties, special-occasion parties, or one-on-one cooking classes. Whatever type of culinary experience the client desires is custom-tailored to the event. Culinary consulting services are provided to food service industry professionals in the form of staff training, kitchen setup, food safety, shift prep checklists, and menu/curriculum development used to train multiple staff members using the same methodology.

**What was your motivation for becoming a chef and/or starting your own business?**

I started this business in order to pursue my true passions — cooking and caring for others! I grew up in Hartford, Connecticut, the youngest of five children. We didn't have a lot of money, but we were rich with the love of our family and the food of our ancestors. I was spoiled in the notion of good food. The neighborhood we lived in was affectionately known as "Little Italy." Every street corner had a different pizza place, Italian restaurant, or bakery. We were lucky enough to partake of these special treats from time to time.

Thankfully, our Mom was an awesome cook who could make delicious meals using the sparsest ingredients. She and our grandmother taught me about the fresh flavors of our Sicilian heritage. As I grew older, I began to cook our family dinner after school each day. These meals revolved around "normal" American and Italian meals. Each Thursday, known as "leftovers night," the creative juices began to fly! I would take the bits of meals left from the previous three days and create (hopefully) a new exotic dish. Most Thursdays were successful, and those that weren't spurred me on to produce something more palatable the next time.

I was lucky to live in an environment that fostered unconditional love, learning, and a focus on helping others. My Mom taught us the importance of treating others as we would like to be treated and to walk the extra mile to help someone out. That has remained ingrained in me and is the true essence of who I am.

During my 23-year career in the US Air Force, I had the opportunity to live in and visit countries around the world. The very people I worked with were my "family" away from home. I used my cooking talent to show my brothers- and sisters-in-arms the love I felt for them. I would learn about the foods of their heritage or region and recreate dishes for special meals, holidays, or celebrations. We shared our life joys, accomplishments, disappointments, and major decisions over food at someone's table.

I recreated dishes we had eaten in Greece, Italy, Saudi Arabia, and many other exotic locations to share the memories we created in those places. The bond we share is lifelong; therefore, I have a "home" in just about every state in America and in many countries abroad. I'm rich in the unconditional love of my family and friends. Giving this love freely through my food and having the ability to help others places me in the self-actualization spectrum. I use my God-given talents for His purpose for my life.

**What was your motivation for becoming a chef and/or starting your own business?**

My motivation to become a chef stemmed from my ability to show love through the meals I created. In 2010, when the Culinary Institute of America (CIA) opened a campus in San Antonio, Texas, I was living in Maryland, working as a consultant for the Department of Defense. I treated myself to a vacation to attend a week-long food enthusiast course. This course was called "basic training"; the focus was the fundamentals of cooking. In four short days, I learned a lot about why I cooked the way I did and how to utilize the new skills and techniques they taught during the class. The seed was planted. I wanted to find a way to move to San Antonio, with the hope of attending the CIA one day.

I was offered a job position and moved to Texas in March 2011. After only two years, I was able to resign my position and begin the culinary arts program. Prior to starting school, I decided to open my personal chef business. I dedicated the business to my mom. Her maiden name was Bonaiuto (bon-eye-u-toe), which literally translates to "good help"! I wanted to honor her and all she gave and taught us. Through this business, I am able to give unconditional love, celebrate special occasions, and create memories for my clients at their own dining table.

**What have you learned about yourself through running your business?**

- Be true to yourself. If something doesn't feel right, listen to your gut.

- Surround yourself with like-minded people who are looking to build you up and help you achieve your goals.

- Align yourself with people who have accomplished what you are striving for.

- Give yourself permission to succeed.

- Humble yourself and ask for help. There are many people who are as ready to help you as you are to help them.

- Have faith in yourself. God gave you the ideas you have because He has a plan to bring them to fruition.

**What three things do you wish you would have known when you started?**

Starting a personal chef business involves more than cooking. You have to have business management tools and knowledge in order to identify your strengths and weaknesses.

- Utilize local resources when setting up your business. I suggest SCORE office mentors. They have a lot of knowledge and are willing to help for free. Let the professionals handle business aspects that you're not proficient at, such as web design, accounting, and marketing.

- Set goals and get out there and do them. You can paralyze yourself into inaction by waiting for the "right" time.

- Create calendar time each week to focus on administrative work such as menu development, responding to clients, invoices, basic accounting, etc.

**Can you share some early challenges in your business career and how you have learned to overcome them?**

Running a business can be daunting at times. Starting out as a personal chef, I was met with the same challenges everyone faces, such as how to price services, how to find a target market, how to advertise appropriately, and how to actually get out there and start cooking! Yes, we all have periods of insecurity about what we're doing. The best step I took was reaching out for help from seasoned professionals. I also attended the national United States Personal Chef Association Conference. The conference is a four-day event filled with classes on every aspect of this business. I left the conference more knowledgeable and feeling more confident about my business.

Getting out and cooking also helped build confidence and reinforced how much I love to cook and why. Get to know other chefs in your area and set up a network of allies.

I have dubbed this past year "the year of experiences." I went through several life-changing events during this time, and I needed to take a look at what I really wanted to do with my business. Fortunately, I've had the luxury of taking advantage of many different food-related opportunities.

- I worked on a friend's food truck serving clientele the company's exclusive fare. This gave me insight to the preparation and product delivery, as well as to the need for a solid system of food cost control and food safety.

- On several occasions, I've worked as a food stylist assistant for a local grocer and a national seafood company. Food styling allowed me the chance to see food from a different perspective and learn some tricks of the trade.

- I once taught a local TV host how to cook. On six separate segments, we prepared healthy meals and special, easy-to-make holidays meals for viewers.

- I enjoy public speaking and had a chance to share my experience at the CIA with the Road Scholars, a seasoned group of travelers who came to our city to learn about its history. On a few other occasions, I demonstrated how to make tamales and relayed the cultural ties to this time-honored tradition.

- I was able to talk about and demonstrate how to create some healthy international snacks for a medical company's public service event.

- Most recently, I was asked by a boutique hotel to accept a position as an on-call sous-chef. This was the result of the work I did for a fundraiser for the Leukemia and Lymphoma Society.

These experiences have opened my eyes to very exciting alternative job opportunities in the food industry.

## What three characteristics describe what has made you successful and why?

*Keep your face always toward the sunshine and the shadows will fall behind you.* — Walt Whitman

I am the eternal optimist. I believe there is a silver lining in every cloud. Although we may encounter disappointments, we need to sit back and consider what we can learn rather than let negativity take over. There is a reason why things work the way they do. Turn the downfalls to your advantage.

I am passionate about what I do. I put my knowledge, skills, and heart into everything. I give back to the community and my colleagues while continuing to learn each and every day.

I am thorough with exhaustive attention to detail, whether I'm planning a menu, creating a training guide, designing a kitchen, or helping another business fulfill its requirements.

**How have you defined your voice in your market?**

I utilize my consulting experience to help businesses create policies and procedures. I also provide them with training and improve the efficiency of their business processes.

I have a large network in my area, and I'm often the conduit for solving staffing needs and providing information for business-to-business solutions. I align people who need each other's services.

I provide a personal touch and encourage my clients to pamper themselves with customized, one-of-a-kind food experiences.

**What would you advise someone who is struggling to build his or her brand?**

Definitely take on a mentor who has been *extremely successful* with his or her business. Find a business coach who will help you clarify your structure and goals and create the steps to get you where you want to be. Use these resources even if you have to pay for them. It's easier and more cost effective to do it right the first time. You will go farther faster without making costly mistakes by trying to do it on your own.

**Staying motivated when things don't seem to be coming together is a challenge at times. How do you motivate yourself? How would you advise someone else?**

When I feel like I'm losing motivation or times are slow, I take advantage of the opportunity for reflection. I remind myself that things might not be coming together because they are not supposed to. Cherishing the down time helps me re-energize. Take a look at what you've been doing and identify where your revenue is coming from. Is that the path you want to continue on?

Each month, when I'm doing my basic accounting, I have a chart at the bottom of the spreadsheet that lists the types of events I've done. I keep a yearly running total so I can see at a glance what streams of income I have. This allows me to see what I've been doing and where I'm generating income. It also allows me to make fact-based decisions on how I can streamline my processes.

**What has been your most effective marketing tool/strategy and why?**

Word-of-mouth referrals have always been my most effective marketing tool. I nurture the relationships I have with industry professionals in town and am continually referred to by these associates. I have received numerous referrals across the spectrum for all of my services. Public speaking is another great way to get yourself out there and become a recognized leader in your industry.

**What do you love most about the industry you are in, and how do you stand out in the crowd?**

This industry gives the opportunity to shine with your talents and care for your clients. I love that I can create great dining experiences for my clients. I also like to see colleagues grow in their businesses, skills, and potential.

I stand out in the crowd by giving back to the community and maintaining a close relationship with the CIA and industry leaders. Volunteering at the CIA affords me the opportunity to stay up to date with trends and with how we as a food community are growing in San Antonio, Texas.

**One of the biggest struggles entrepreneurs have is how to price themselves. What advice would you share about pricing your services and offerings?**

Pricing is often one of the most difficult areas. There's always the desire to price lower than you should. Identify your target market and get to that market. You are offering an exceptional service and deserve to be paid well.

One of the easiest ways to price yourself is to create a budget to identify how much money you need to pay your bills and make a profit. Once you have that monthly figure, you can work backward from there to decide what you need to charge. This takes away the uncertainty of "Am I worth that much?"

Check with other personal chefs in your area and find out their pricing structure. Sometimes you can find their range by checking their websites. Make sure to price your services separately from the cost of groceries. This will help you not to stress yourself out trying to buy the best ingredients at the lowest cost. At the end of the day, value yourself and the service you provide. Target the people who can afford your services and stick to your guns.

**What advice would you give to a chef entrepreneur who is ready to take his or her business to the next level?**

- Ensure you are making decisions based on facts (data) that you've compiled over time.

- Work with a proven mentor who has been successful in business for many years. He or she will be happy to help you grow and succeed.

- Run your ideas by a select group to find out how those people have handled challenges and to see if your next planned steps have been tried before.

**What "must-have" resources would you recommend someone use in his or her business?**

- Running a personal chef business takes a lot more than knowing how to cook. You are a chef. Are you also an accountant, website designer, and marketing guru? Find reliable agents who can do their best work for you so that you can focus on your strengths.

- Collaborate with other chefs in your area so that you have a network to turn to when you are booked, are overbooked, or need help. Knowing the talents and specialties of your colleagues can help with your schedule and can help ensure client satisfaction.

## What makes you a chef who is making an impact?

I work within my value system. Helping others is my greatest asset, and this allows me the chance to give regardless of any reciprocation. Creating a cohesive environment helps everyone to be the best they can be. Creating an atmosphere of giving with your colleagues enlightens each one of you.

## What is your favorite part about running your business?

My favorite part of my business is making people happy by doing what I love — helping people, whether an individual, a business, or a colleague. Knowing that I can make someone's day a bit brighter because of the solutions I provide is rewarding.

## What do you do for work/life balance and to take care of yourself?

- I work out at least three times a week. Working out helps motivate me to be the best I can in all areas of my life. I get a surge of energy that helps each day be productive and thoughtful. Creativity thrives with the adrenaline push of each workout.

- I take the time to cook for myself so I have meals available after cooking for others.

- I take time out with friends and family to reconnect and socialize.

**Wildcard question! Share whatever you would like the reader to know about you, your business, or your journey. Tell us your story.**

In any endeavor you partake in, do your best. You have the resources, knowledge, and answers within. Have faith in yourself and your abilities. Exude confidence even when you're not feeling it! Give back to your community and to others. *Go for it!*

# Continue the Conversation with
# Chef Tracey Callahan:

 Tracey Callahan is a classically trained Chef from The Culinary Institute of America. Her love for cooking began as a child in the south end of Hartford, Connecticut's "Little Italy" and continued during her 23-year career in the US Air Force. Having traveled across the globe to various countries she gained an appreciation for local cuisines. She has tied her passion for food, travel, and helping others by sharing authentic cuisine with her clients, family and friends.

In August 2010 she was recognized for her talents by winning an "Iron Chef" type competition on board the inaugural Celebrity Cruise Line/Food Network Eastern Caribbean cruise. Chefs Cat Cora and Aaron Sanchez were two of the judges for the event. "It was the opportunity of a lifetime."

Tracey has a B.S. of Business Management from National Louis University, an A.S. of Culinary Arts from The Culinary Institute of America, an A.S. in Communications Technology from the Community College of the Air Force. She is also a graduate of The Culinary Business Academy and is a member of the United States Personal Chef Association and Women Chefs and Restaurateurs.

**Website:**
www.thegoodhelper.com

# CHEF WALDA COLLINS
## Founder, AlignMint Culinary Services

**Share with us what your business is and why you wanted to start this business.**

Strategic AlignMint Culinary Services equips and empowers its clients to experience an attainable, happier, healthier lifestyle. It's about bringing people full circle — creating nutritional strategies that align the mind, body, and spirit.

Whether I'm cooking, educating, or training, I love to see people live, love, learn, and grow into healthier beings. Being "healthy" is not just having what looks good on the outside. It's a whole-person concept. As triune beings, we are out of sync if we don't obtain that three-fold alignment.

My journey began long before I knew I wanted to be a chef. In fact, I once stayed as far away from the kitchen as I could. But I did observe from afar. I was not that child you saw at Mama's or Grandma's side with a spoon or spatula. I didn't want to cook. I didn't want to wash dishes. I just wanted to taste the end product that my Grandma crafted — the soulful food that drew everyone in for more. I know my Grandmother is looking down from above, cheering me on, saying, "that's my Waulie." Yeah, she never called me by my name! She was an amazing cook! But I also have to give credit to my mom, all of my aunts, and even my uncles, because they all have a knack for whipping up something good in the kitchen. Gravy runs deep in our veins.

As a young person, my best therapy was loud music, headphones, and my inner space. This space was a place of healing for me (along with the food, of course). It was a place deep within, where I could tune out all my surroundings and create my own environment of peace.

By the time I reached high school (at the High School for Health Professions, where I studied nursing and interned in hospitals), I knew I had compassion for people. Oddly enough, nursing required more blood and guts than I had the stomach for, so I made a drastic turn. I wanted something more. I was timid and shy, and I knew I needed to get beyond that to be successful. So what did I do?

I joined the United States Marine Corps, the toughest branch of military service. Wow! What a different world! It was on this journey that my life began to take shape. I grew. I learned. I was challenged. I was disciplined. I understood the concepts of team and lifelong friendships. Many times, this camaraderie was developed around the table, in each other's homes, at cookouts, and even in field training evolutions. Food. Fun. Laughter. It was an extension of family that was all too familiar.

While serving as a Marine and sharing a great deal of my life with fellow Marines, I learned how powerful food really is. Whether we exchanged recipes or swapped field rations, it all revolved around food as the epicenter. Food has the power to heal and make a not-so-good situation better. Not only did I recognize the power of food, but I knew how to cook! Go figure!

When I cook, an atmosphere is created that causes people to gather around in laughter. Food is powerful. Food is imagination, and presentation is everything. The look, the feel, and the aroma of good food is magically healing. However, I like to cook on the healthier side because food is medicine. It heals and aligns the body. Hippocrates once famously said, "Let food be thy medicine and medicine be thy food."

Before I finished culinary school, I began a whole new journey to complete my calling. I was called into ministry in 2010, prior to making my last deployment to Afghanistan. I was probably called before then, but that's when I answered. I didn't know what to do from there. I returned from deployment, then back to my family in the United States from Okinawa, Japan, and I followed my intuition. Well, it wasn't quite that easy. I struggled to transition from the military and find my place in the civilian sector. I loved making cupcakes; it was the "in" thing at the time. So I followed my heart and went to culinary school. But that cupcake thing . . . it didn't line up with my calling. Besides, my health was taking a drastic turn.

With the scare of high blood pressure and diabetes, it didn't take me long to realize that cupcakes weren't the path I wanted to take. So I juggled ministry and culinary. I shared this with a friend in culinary school, wondering how to handle being both a minister and a chef. I thought that the two professions were on totally opposite ends of the spectrum. Her response was, "Oh, you're going to heal people through food." I kind of got it, but I didn't.

I began to more fully understand when I started receiving requests for help! Before I knew it, I had a client with Lupus. Then another plea came from a client with a long history of heart disease, then another from a woman who wanted assistance with her weight. Suddenly, the light bulb came on! The testimonials and praise reports from these clients all told me that I was healing people through food.

My life as a personal chef and healthy life strategist has catapulted me along my journey of health and wellness as I help others strategically align their lives through food and nutrition.

**What was your motivation for becoming a chef and/or starting your own business?**

Even if no one else will, I believe in myself. I bring all my gifts and talents to the table, and there's value in all of them. I believe we are all uniquely created and have a purpose by which we were made. My passion is my purpose!

A renowned pastor and best-selling author, Bishop T.D. Jakes, once said, "If you can't figure out your purpose, figure out your passion. For your passion will lead you right into your purpose." As a chef, I am innovative and share my passion, knowledge, and expertise with many in order to see them live a healthier lifestyle. No matter the capacity, I find myself giving back to others.

I've worked in several restaurants, and that lifestyle is limiting in so many ways. It doesn't give you the same drive to live out your God-given purpose. Nor does it pay you your worth. My creativity flourishes when I'm not limited in any specific way. Starting my own business allowed me to be flexible and creative, yet it challenged me to be disciplined. You would think that discipline would come easily for someone who spent 23 years as a Marine. The Marine Corps taught me a lot. It was my life. I lived, laughed, and, most importantly, learned. I learned that I could be whatever I wanted to be. But I also learned that there is a cost; there is a sacrifice.

Becoming a chef and starting my own business is not my end all; it's another step on my journey.

**What have you learned about yourself through running your business?**

Being an entrepreneur has its ups and downs. However, a phase comes in which you learn more and more about yourself. I have discovered that being an entrepreneur is not for everyone. It takes guts and tenacity to really be successful. I have also learned that, in this whole evolution of becoming an entrepreneur, I need to trust myself. I may not have 100% of the answers, but it's better to have 80% than to try to be perfect. Trust what you know!

**What three things do you wish you would have known when you started?**

There are three things that I consider critical now that I'm in this game. I wasn't well-versed in these things before I started. They are:

1. Resources
2. A team
3. A plan

*Resources* are a necessity in any business venture. There are several resources a business needs to succeed: A) financial, B) physical, C) human, and D) educational.

*A team* helps you carry out the mission and goals of the business. You can't do it all yourself. Surround yourself with people who have drive, determination, and enthusiasm.

*A plan* gives you direction and helps you and everyone else know where the business is going. It's your map. I like to think I'm not one who has to know everything or has to have everything mapped out before I start. With a great idea and a little direction, I jump in with both feet. That can be dangerous! But I'd rather start before I'm ready than not start at all.

**Can you share some early challenges in your business career and how you have learned to overcome them?**

Early on, I struggled to find where I belonged. I asked myself, "Where do I fit in this culinary world?" One thing I knew was that success wouldn't come if I stood still. So as I took steps forward, I saw growth almost immediately. You just have to get started. However, you can't be everything to everybody (as I quickly learned)! You have to find your sweet spot.

There are three C's in life and business that lead to greatness: challenge, change, and commitment. My business challenged me to step up or step away. I knew that if I stepped away, I'd consider myself a quitter or a failure. Marines don't do that! Many days I asked myself, "Why should I continue to do this? It's too much work!" My resolve came from the fact that I wasn't doing this for me, but for the many lives that would be changed as I walked out my purpose.

Many people despise change. It leads us into the unpredictable. It exposes our weaknesses. But I had to embrace the change — the transition into this new life and new career after serving so many years in the Marine Corps. What I've learned in business is that change, if accepted, will turn us in the right direction and send us soaring to new heights. My compassion for people and my love for being a chef have allowed me to remain committed. Commitment is the glue that helps us overcome the challenges and changes we face in this business.

**What three characteristics describe what has made you successful and why?**

1. Passion
2. Vision
3. Conviction

These characteristics motivate me to focus forward, upward, and outward — forward toward my goals and my future, upward to encourage others to reach for their dreams, and outward to give back (including mentoring and coaching).

**How have you defined your voice in your market?**

I don't cook; I create and innovate. I don't only create food; I create the atmosphere, the presentation, the ambiance, and a sense of belonging.

I coach, communicate, and care. I "strategically align" and empower my audience, readers, and clients to grow and explore creative benefits for their overall health.

I come from a long line of educators, ministers, and entrepreneurs. Educating and engaging my audience creatively and passionately continues to reflect excellence and helps me stand out in my market.

**What would you advise someone who is struggling to build his or her brand?**

If I knew of someone who was struggling in this area, I would tell that person to look at his or her "why" list:

1. What would you like to accomplish?
2. Who is your audience?
3. How can you make someone feel your brand?
4. Would you do this even if you did not get paid?
5. What do you want your company to be remembered for?

Being able to answer these questions will help you focus on your "why" and motivate you during the struggle.

**Staying motivated when things don't seem to be coming together is a challenge at times. How do you motivate yourself? How would you advise someone else?**

Running is one of my all-time motivators. I love to run, but sometimes I have to push myself. That same impetus is what helps me remember the benefits of running. I find clarity, energy, and a second wind when I push myself to run.

When I push myself with my business, I find the strategy and the results are similar — I gain defined clarity, renewed energy, and a second wind to take me to the next level.

My advice, dear friend, is to find what motivates you and gives you that feeling that you "can do all things" through Him who gives you strength!

**What has been your most effective marketing tool/strategy and why?**

My most effective marketing tool is word-of-mouth advertising through corporate events, church gatherings, social clubs, co-workers, family, and friends.

Word-of-mouth advertising is tested, true evidence from someone who has experienced your services. However, when referrals stop coming in, the next best source is being "present." Get in the public eye — network and share with others at cooking demonstrations, health fairs, and local events.

However, within the structures of print, electronic, social, and radio/TV media lie strategically essential elements of marketing. If these elements are at work, you as a small business owner will save energy, time, and money.

**What do you love most about the industry you are in, and how do you stand out in the crowd?**

I love creating my recipes and bending the rules — creating new rules and tastes that delight my audience and leave them asking for more. Standing out in the crowd is not something I do intentionally. However, it's caused that passion and drive of going above and beyond the norm, which is my pursuit of excellence. I always take my meals just one step past my competition in quality, service, and presentation. I have confidence in knowing that the food is great, but that my service to my clients is even greater.

**One of the biggest struggles entrepreneurs have is how to price themselves. What advice would you share about pricing your services and offerings?**

Don't be afraid to charge your worth! Your training and education weren't free, and neither are your services. In some senses, people find value in higher pricing. Be proud but not arrogant. Always remember to cover your costs, and give yourself permission to be paid for taking the time to invest in yourself and your future.

Undoubtedly, my clients get the better deal because I far exceed their expectations.

**What advice would you give to a chef entrepreneur who is ready to take his or her business to the next level?**

Pray, plan, and pursue. Don't allow yourself to be bitten by "paralysis analysis." Start before you're ready. We waste a lot of time getting started, or we never start because we're "getting ready." You don't need to know it all, but you do need a plan in place. Write down your vision, then run with it. Yes, challenges will come. Yes, there will be changes. But remember that your commitment and your resolve are yours to help others.

1. Create space to find clarity.
2. Surround yourself with people who can see your vision and can give you genuine, valuable insight.
3. Think BIG (Bold, Ingenious, Great)

**What "must-have" resources would you recommend someone use in his or her business?**

It may not seem like a resource, but the biggest "must-have" is investing. Invest in yourself. Stay up to date with resources in this industry — such as newsletters, journals, and websites — that provide the latest information on improving your business. In addition, attend conferences and workshops and join business associations to sharpen your skills. Learning is continuous and ongoing.

**What makes you a chef who is making an impact?**

I believe I'm making an impact as a chef because I'm on a mission. I recognize this as a calling that is much bigger than me. I believe the impact I am to have in my community and the world draws me to the next phase, prepares me for what's to come, and propels me to greater heights. I am not only pulled higher, but I am taken deeper into creative thought.

**What is your favorite part about running your business?**

As I've stated earlier, I am a very creative person. Having the ability to think "outside the box" drives my passion. Creativity gives me an unexplained energy. Being able to use that creativity and flexibility in my business makes me that much more effective and efficient.

**What do you do for work/life balance and to take care of yourself?**

My work/life balance comes much easier now that I'm an empty nester. I can't say that I had much balance when I was a young mom, wife, and Marine. I have always been a nurturer —always yielding my time for others. Running has always been and still continues to be my outlet. However, I also realize that you have to get to a point where you turn everything off, put everything away, allow nothing to fill your mind or your space, and just breathe. Try it: just take in a deep breath and hold it for a count of seven, then slowly exhale. Inhale again, hold, and exhale. Do this about five times and you'll feel much better, even in the midst of a crazy, chaotic day. I call that my mini getaway.

Balancing work and life can be a little tricky. If you lean too much one way or another, you'll find yourself out of sorts. One thing that keeps me in perfect peace is my relationship with God. I feel it's vitally important to have a spiritual connection.

True balance comes when we have healthy relationships, a career we love, some level of physical activity, and spiritual nutrition. In these you'll find a happier and healthier, mind, body, and spirit.

**Wildcard question! Share whatever you would like the reader to know about you, your business, or your journey. Tell us your story.**

My journey has been nothing short of ins and outs, twists and turns, highs and lows. But through it all, I have had the best "ride or die" partner. He's my cheerleader, supporter, sounding board, and, at times, even my battering board. God knew just whom I needed in my life to keep me grounded when I get too high or to be an encourager when I get too low. I'm grateful to God for my two sons, Zachary and Keith, Jr. But most importantly, I'm proud to be a part of the life of my dear friend and husband, Dr. Keith G. Collins.

I'd like to leave you with this. You are uniquely and wonderfully made. You have been given this gift and passion for cooking, not only for yourself, but to help someone else. Walk boldly! Be encouraged! Know that the thing that you're passionate about is your purpose. Live it out loud; you are created for purpose!

# Continue the Conversation with Chef Walda Collins:

Walda Collins is a retired Marine and three-time Combat Veteran, turned Personal Chef and Healthy Life Strategist. Founder of Strategic AlignMint Culinary Services, Walda is located in the beautiful Hill Country of San Antonio, TX.

Upon retirement from the Marines, Walda transitioned from "Guns to Gourmet", utilizing her skills, which allowed her culinary innovation to morph into a method of identifying and creating nutritional strategies. Her tactical creativity equips and empowers her clients to experience an attainable, happier, healthier lifestyle through food, nutrition and health coaching, while obtaining a three-fold alignment of mind, body and spirit.

Walda is a member of *Sistas in Business, Christian Women's Small Business Association, and the United States Personal Chef Association.* She is a consummate professional, as well as a volunteer for the *American Heart Association,* educating the community on the benefits of being heart healthy. Walda is also a graduate of the International Culinary School at the Art Institute, CFCI Bible Institute and currently attending the Institute for Integrative Nutrition.

Walda is an inspirational speaker that not only motivates, but challenges her target market to make life-changing transformations. She has been featured on *News4 San Antonio, Dallas High Life TV & Radio, Uniquely Designed Talk Radio, Christian Women's Small Business Association, Sista's In Business* and a host of other platforms.

**Website:**
www.strategicalignmint.com

# CHEF ALICIA OJEDA
## Chef – Educator - Consultant

**Share with us what your business is and why you wanted to start this business.**

I created my first culinary business in the early 1990's. I realized that I had a natural ability and passion for feeding — nourishing — people with delicious foods at a variety of events that left them with incredible memories! Long before it was "trendy," I used fresh, wholesome ingredients and prepared everything from scratch.

**What was your motivation for becoming a chef and/or starting your own business?**

When I originally started my full-service catering business, I soon realized that I *loved* creating an *extraordinary experience . . . from soup to nuts!* Whether a chamber luncheon, an elaborate wedding and reception, or an HRC fundraiser, I loved it all!

Most food I personally tasted at events was mediocre at best. I was determined to provide absolute deliciousness one plate at a time! While attending a two-year culinary program at Long Beach City College so that I could continue to run my business, I was a "sponge." I also took ProChef Series classes and attended specialty conferences at the Culinary Institute of America in St. Helena, California. There I had the opportunity to meet and learn from internationally acclaimed chef/author Paula Wolfert, chef/restaurateur Mai Pham, and many more! To round out my experience, I completed my internship at world-renowned chef Michel Richard's Citrus and Horn Blower Dining Yachts. Soon after, I began my career with Bon Appétit Management Company, where owner Fedele Bauccio described me as the "most passionate chef" he knew! (That's saying a lot!)

**What have you learned about yourself through running your business?**

Save money for taxes! Have a good bookkeeper, and don't try to do your own taxes and bookkeeping! I have learned so much about myself — what my strengths are and that I don't have to do it all; it's okay to ask for help. I have learned that I love teaching and that I am a good leader. I have learned that being an entrepreneur/solopreneur is not easy, and that it really takes something to stay motivated and keep a forward vision. I have learned that the "devil is in the detail" and the importance of being picky, both with hiring and taking on clients. I have also learned the art of saying "No." The lesson of self-care and nourishing myself is critical!

**What three things do you wish you would have known when you started?**

I wish I had known that *vision* is everything. Creating a vision for what I wish to create in my business is my true north, my compass. (I am not necessarily speaking of "goals.") My vision helps keep me aligned with who I am, what's important to me, and what I want to create for myself and my business. It helps me focus on these things instead of on chasing "dollars" and taking on projects that only pay bills but do not move my business forward.

I also wish I had known that it will all turn out; there are no mistakes/failures, but only continual learning — opportunities for growth and expansion. I get to learn from everyone and every situation that comes across my path. Each past experience has brought me to this moment. How I choose to frame it can either serve me or deplete me — it's my choice!

Finally, I wish I had known the importance of finding time for play, fun, and travel! I have had major periods of "workaholicism" — nose to the grindstone; an old paradigm of "work, work, work." It gets old, and it's more important to work smartly and make use of all the modern conveniences of the world wide web. My reach extends much farther now that I combine online efforts with my physical business. Electronic products can have a far-reaching effect, much more so than the effect I can have by myself.

**Can you share some early challenges in your business career and how you have learned to overcome them?**

The biggest challenge in this incarnation of my business is "chasing dollars" and just getting by. So instead, in 2015 (it's taken that long!), I finally hired a coach/mentor. I wish I would have made this investment years ago. It is very difficult for us to see ourselves and our own blind spots. My business coach has been like rear view and side view mirrors for me, illuminating my blind spots, nudging me, encouraging me, supporting me, etc.

Joining a group of peers has also been super helpful. We brainstorm to create solutions for existing problems, and we network with one another. We collaborate and support each with our own unique flares.

**What three characteristics describe what has made you successful and why?**

1. Passion

I am a foodie at heart. My love and passion for food has never waned; it has merely evolved to fruits, especially the tropical exotics like durian, jackfruit, mango, mamey sapote, mangosteen, and many others! I delight in introducing people to the glorious flavors, aromas, textures, and colors of these succulent gifts from nature. As the seasons ebb and flow, each brings its bounty in glorious perfection. Freshly picked vegetables and exquisitely ripe fruits are decadent in their natural state and require only the subtlest preparation. They are "simply delicious" all on their own!

## 2. Innovation

People often ask me if I feel limited working almost exclusively with fresh fruits and vegetables. In reality, I have the *entire* produce section at my disposal! What's more, a single ingredient, such as a mango, an apple, or a melon, often comes in a cornucopia of varieties — if you know where to look.

Over the years, I have translated the basics I learned so long ago into one-of-a-kind signature dishes that accentuate the flavors that burst forth from the ingredients from which they are made. Rather than seeking to mimic meat-based dishes, I create masterpieces that celebrate fruits and veggies for what they are.

Unlike gourmet-style raw-food chefs, I refrain from using salt, oils, alliums, or stimulating seasonings and spices in my cuisine, yet I still manage to create perfectly balanced flavors and textures. I sometimes employ a dehydrator, which provides additional variety of texture, and I occasionally make judicious use of whole-food fats in small quantities, crafting "celebration foods" for those in transition. After all, it's not what we do once in a while that matters; it's what we do every day that gives us our present experience.

## 3. Commitment

When I count backward and realize that I have been in the "industry" since the early 1990's, I am surprised at how long I have been a chef. It rarely feels like work. I am eager and enthusiastic to enjoy the years ahead of me, knowing that my craft will help many more people heal their bodies and reverse chronic and often "untreatable" conditions with scrumptious, life-giving foods. I have devoted my career to enriching the lives of others, bringing them ease, inspiration, and radiant health through a whole-food, plant-based diet.

**How have you defined your voice in your market?**

I don't believe I actually have one. Most of what I have done has been through word of mouth. So I am just beginning to find a voice. It definitely has not been my strength.

**What would you advise someone who is struggling to build his or her brand?**

Get it on paper — the old fashioned way. Describe it. Draw it out. Decide what you want to be known for and remembered by. How do you want to influence and impact people? Be *really, really, really* clear on that. Get creative and use big paper and colored pencils — have fun with it. Check out a tool called "mind mapping," then look to have someone help you with it. Stay true to your message.

**Staying motivated when things don't seem to be coming together is a challenge at times. How do you motivate yourself? How would you advise someone else?**

I have always been a "glass half full" person. The lens with which we look at things is *our choice.* Start the morning and end each day with a focus on what *is* working and going well. Any time you find yourself getting into that negative space or dwelling on feelings of hopelessness, pause, take a breath, and shift your attention to something you are grateful for. Sometimes we need to start generally (it has to be believable, however). This technique is also called "imagination activation exercise." Close your eyes and imagine yourself already experiencing the win or success you desire. Get as detailed as possible. How do you feel? Who are you with? What are some of the things your clients are saying to you? Continue to keep your vision alive. Vision boards also work very well with a collage of pictures that evoke certain feelings from you regarding your business.

**What has been your most effective marketing tool/strategy and why?**

Word of mouth. Each person who tastes your food is a potential billboard, business card, etc.

**What do you love most about the industry you are in, and how do you stand out in the crowd?**

What I love most is the opportunity I have to empower people to nourish themselves in a way that truly promotes their health and is satisfying on a very deep level. I stand out in that I "work myself out of a job" for many of my private clients. I teach them various techniques and methods instead of delivering prepared foods or just teaching them recipes. I get them so comfortable with certain methods that they can then create their own variations, really learn flavor balancing, and produce *delicious* staple items to use throughout the week in their meals.

**One of the biggest struggles entrepreneurs have is how to price themselves. What advice would you share about pricing your services and offerings?**

Many personal chefs and restaurateurs who are just starting out make the same mistake: because they don't know their numbers, they price blindly. I think it is essential both to set the initial price correctly and to keep that price up as seasons change and prices fluctuate. There are so many programs available now, such as ChefTec, that make the process easy.

As a personal chef, I believe it is essential to value yourself and your time and charge accordingly. When you spend a day away from your home office, what wage do you want to earn "just to leave your home"? Be confident in your pricing and know that you can command a specific wage.

**What advice would you give to a chef entrepreneur who is ready to take his or her business to the next level?**

I have mentioned this before, but it bears repeating: hire a coach/mentor/consultant that you resonate with to help uncover your blind spots and support you in realizing your vision.

**What "must-have" resources would you recommend someone use in his or her business?**

- Networking with peers or other chefs in the industry (organizations like WCR, ACF, etc.)
- Staying current with ongoing education and food trends
- Working on personal development
- Attending quality networking events
- Acquiring a mentor/business coach
- Acquiring a virtual assistant/marketing support/social media support

**What makes you a chef who is making an impact?**

I feed hundreds from all over the world, and I travel internationally, as well. I travel not only as a chef for events, but also to teach people "how to" so that they are inspired and empowered to create delicious, life-enhancing meals and dishes when they return to their own kitchens. More than this, I bring love into kitchens. The smells, flavors, and textures of food have the potential to evoke emotions and memories.

When my large extended family gathered at my abuelita's house, she always prepared food for us. I remember how she would stand at her tiny stove, lovingly preparing tacos, tortas, caldos, and so on. As each family member arrived, she continued to prepare something delicious for each one. We never went hungry. She used simple, humble, whole ingredients — potatoes, beans, rice, corn, chiles, and so on. I believe very much that the energy, love, and care she cheerfully put into the food was the life force we felt as we enjoyed it with appreciation and gratitude. It was *delicious!*

Whether I am preparing for 600 with a team of volunteers at the WFF or for a private client, I, too, infuse my food with positive love energy — prana. Foods prepared with love taste sublime indeed!

**What is your favorite part about running your business?**

There are so many things I love about running my own business, but several things stand out. I love that I get to contribute and make a difference for people, either through meals I prepare or through hands-on classes I teach. These classes help my clients feel *really* empowered and inspired when they return to their own kitchens. I also get to create amazing "aha" moments when people taste my food and then realize that it's completely free of allergens and has been prepared with truly healthful "cooking techniques."

I also enjoy the freedom of scheduling my time so that I can spend extended family time with my grandchildren.

**What do you do for work/life balance and to take care of yourself?**

I think it is essential to manage stress. I have a daily meditation practice, and I practice yoga and take daily walks. I also have an hourly alarm set on my phone to remind me to breathe and check in — to ask myself, "What am I present to? What am I grateful for?"

**Wildcard question! Share whatever you would like the reader to know about you, your business, or your journey. Tell us your story.**

I have *loved* being a chef; I couldn't imagine doing anything else! Leading up to 2002, when I became a vegan, I was a staunch carnivore. I had *zero* intention of ever considering a vegan diet, let alone a raw one! I thought I was merely going to learn a new "cuisine." It came as a complete surprise to me that, after two weeks of eating this way, I felt so *amazing* — like never before. The transformational experience I had was incredible, so I decided to take it on as my own lifestyle. I experienced an overwhelming sense of peace and well-being, and I felt compelled to share this with others.

We live in a time in which people are waking up to the fact that what we put into our bodies has a direct effect on our health. "Food as medicine" is a philosophy that is spreading quickly as people are tiring of not feeling well and/or being told that nothing can be done, or that they have to be on a specific medication for life!

When given the proper "fuel," our bodies are capable of true healing. The "fake foods" of the fast food industry are diminishing in popularity, and people are coming back to eating "whole *real* foods," which can be absolutely delicious.

This is a time of much worldwide disease and ill health. As chefs and preparers of food, we can no longer deny the direct correlation between individuals' health and what we put on their plates.

Make every meal count. Choose "real" ingredients. Choose *life-giving* foods. Skip meat and dairy even just one day a week and see how absolutely amazing you can feel. Join me on this healing journey, and enjoy life every day!

# Continue the Conversation with Chef Alicia Ojeda:

 Alicia's classic culinary career spans 25 years, including her roles as executive chef at DreamWorks Studios and chef manager at Sony Music for Bon Appétit Management Company (both in Southern California), as well as Executive Chef at Beets Café, Austin, Texas.

She was inspired to start her own business after experiencing more than 40 pounds of weight loss and regaining control of her health on a raw food diet. Now she helps organizations, professionals, and individuals enjoy the benefits of raw foods through her business consulting, educational courses, and private chef services. She also educates culinary students at Austin's Natural Epicurean Academy of Culinary Arts, where she developed the raw foods curriculum.

When not serving clients or teaching culinary skills, Alicia serves as executive chef at the annual Woodstock Fruit Festival, travels internationally as a retreat chef and raw food educator, and helps chefs expand their wholesome cooking techniques.

Website: www.rawchefalicia.com

# CHEF DONNA BARROW

**Founder**

**Your Plate or Mine, Inc. and Delectables by Donna**

**Share with us what your business is and why you wanted to start this business.**

I own and operate a personal chef business named Your Plate or Mine, which I incorporated in 2009. I focus on three primary areas: at-home dinner parties (as well as special occasions and casual events like breakfasts, brunches, and lunches), dinner solution packages (meals prepared and packaged on-site weekly, bimonthly, or monthly), and interactive cooking parties/cooking lessons.

I started this business because, for as long as I can remember, I wanted to cook for a living. I wanted to drop out of college and work for Club Med, become a chef at a restaurant at age 21, then operate a cute little bistro. However, after my mother strongly shared her opinions, I instead finished school, became an educator, raised a daughter, and worked in my career for 23 years. During those years, I was a home cook; I gave dinner parties, made delicious food for potlucks, and took a few recreational cooking classes, all while honing my technique in seasoning and recreating recipes. I read cookbooks and watched chefs on PBS, then discovered the Food Network in the late 90's. I watched the shows for the techniques and unique tips the TV personalities shared.

A few years after my daughter graduated from college, I began revisiting the idea of becoming a chef. Would I need to go to culinary school? Where would I begin working as a chef? As an educator and lifelong learner, I liked the thought of taking classes. I researched culinary schools and programs and decided on a local professional program that was economically prudent, designed for people who worked full time, and had connections for job placement. I even had a chef coat and textbooks! I was so excited.

I appreciated learning the basic culinary skills and terms that were the basis of much of the food my grandmothers, mother, and aunts prepared, as well as of the food I learned to make. I enjoyed connecting Pommes Anna with my awesome home-style potatoes and understanding that the sauce for my highly requested macaroni and cheese started with a Béchamel. In fact, I loved everything about the mother sauces.

After I completed the program, and while I was still working full time in my career, I needed a way to use my new paid-for culinary skills. So I began catering. It was a disaster! Not the cooking part per se, but lugging chaffers and decorations and organizing the place settings just got in the way of creating delicious food. I was not as organized as I needed to be, and I certainly did not have enough help. Neither did I find fulfillment in making chicken breasts on a budget for 100 people. I discovered that while I had cooked for people for most of my life, I had not "catered" to anyone in that way. My cooking was much more personal and individualized. I did not understand it at the time, but I had been groomed to be a personal chef (PC).

In 2006, my internet searches for "chef careers" yielded the typical results: "restaurant executive chef" (including "sous-chef" and "prep cook"), "caterer," and "private chef." However, "personal chef" popped up as well. I read the descriptions provided by the official associations, and I was initially completely turned off! It sounded too much like domestic work. But three years later, after a few horrible catering gigs and a review of the PC descriptions with a fresh mindset, I realized that being a personal chef was exactly what I wanted. It would mean multiple clients, my own business in which I would set the work style, and opportunities to use my talents for multiple streams of income. In April 2009, I joined the United States Personal Chef Association (USPCA) and incorporated YPOM. I resigned from my "W-2 job" in June, and I flew to New Orleans that summer to attend the USPCA Conference. There I participated in workshops centered around the business of running a PC operation, and I connected with enthusiastically helpful chef mentors. I began cooking for my first clients that August, and I have been cooking for them every other week for going on seven years!

My mother made food for people all the time. She showed love by delivering creative bundles of home-cooked goodness to people's front doors to make their lives a bit easier. She lovingly made dishes such as fried chicken tenders and cornbread sticks, Taco Night fixings, etc. This is the basis for my business: home-cooked goodness prepared and ready for you, just the way you want it, to make your life a little easier. While I am now paid to cook, I still do it with love and pure joy.

**What was your motivation for becoming a chef and/or starting your own business?**

Immediately following my college graduation, I gave birth to my daughter and began my career in public education as a teacher, administrator, and HR assistant director. I didn't think about cooking as a career for a long time, but the desire resurged in the mid-2000's. My mother passed away in 2007, the same year my daughter graduated from college. Those two events — a life cut short and the end of one phase of parenting — caused me to think about what I wanted to do — I mean *really do* for the rest of my life. The 10-year-old Donna reminded me that I wanted to be a chef!

So at age 47, I decided I would become a chef. While I was up to the challenge of working long hours, there was no way I was working the line at a restaurant cutting onions for 16 hours! My experience as an administrator/assistant director in human resources prepared me to be my own boss.

**What have you learned about yourself through running your business?**

I learned to articulate and operate within my personal "work style." I am not a "hustler." I have never had to be *scrappy* to get paid. I have the mentality of a salaried employee with a static, regular paycheck. I had to figure out a way to run my business in a way that mimicked the style with which I was most comfortable.

**What three things do you wish you would have known when you started?**

*Learn accounting* (number one with a bullet!). I wish I had taken a basic course in QuickBooks just to set up my chart of accounts, preferably with an instructor capable of sharing insights to invoicing, tax structures, and more.

Learn marketing, particularly branding.

Start with a list of folks (through social media, email, etc.) and ask people who know you and like you to share information about you.

**Can you share some early challenges in your business career and how you have learned to overcome them?**

As many who have started second careers can probably understand, my first challenge was the drastic drop in salary. It actually fell to no salary; I was just paid as I worked. No more sick time and no vacation balance. Instead, I went to the bank to deposit checks two and three times a week! (Before I began my business, I had not been into a bank for 15 years thanks to direct deposit and online banking). I'm not sure that I've completely overcome these challenges yet, but I now understand/build in/use online payment options, I've built a client base, and I've worked a mixture of jobs that pay in various ways (corporate culinary instructor positions as well as PC jobs).

From the very beginning, I made the decision to incorporate my business to separate and protect myself financially, and with a plan to hire other chefs to work the business (a client hires Your Plate or Mine, not Chef Donna). I began taking on independent contractors to help supplement the income. I finally enrolled the company with the state of California, became an official employer, and began operating payroll as an employee of my own company. This has helped tremendously to provide a steadier personal income. It has also helped to greatly reduce the personal tax debt I owe each April.

I was always used to working in a team environment with staff meetings, lunches out, etc. When I began cooking for clients in their homes, I was alone almost all the time. Then I would go to my home office to work alone. Granted, I had/have a business partner (whose areas of strength are business processes) that was crucial to the process and success of YPOM. We emailed, texted, and talked on the phone regularly, but it was not the same as working in an office with a team of folks in the same career. Eventually, I connected with the USPCA and other chef networking groups, culinary instructors, and small business owners in the culinary field to discuss the specific challenges, goals, and trends of the industry. These relationships helped to mitigate the solitude.

## What three characteristics describe what has made you successful and why?

Adaptive/Adaptable — Things come up. Clients change their minds. Extra guests show up at a barbeque who are gluten-free vegans. Rain comes. Stoves stop working. I always try to roll up my sleeves and go with the flow. I also have a friendly face and a bright smile that seems to put people at ease.

Enthusiastic/Happy — I love what I do! And I spread the joy to those around me like my clients, cooking class students, demonstration audience members, social media contacts, friends, and family.

Intelligent/Knowledgeable — As far as dealing with the human nature, my experience in HR helps me read people. While I generally see the good in all people, I can tell when a client is "just shopping" or if my services aren't what he or she really needs. I can also very quickly determine which chef best matches the needs and personality of each client.

I also know food. When I ask clients questions in order to customize their menu, I can ascertain ingredients based on odd and vague answers. Once, as I was adding brownies to the menu for a client, he asked me to "add a few nuts to make them a little crunchy." When I asked him which nuts he would like, he responded, "Never eat nuts. They should not add flavor like peanuts would do." I then knew to keep the pieces small and to avoid walnuts because their flavor is usually strong. I used chopped pecans, and he was delighted.

**How have you defined your voice in your market?**

I keep it personal. Personal chefs are now in competition with all sorts of meal delivery companies that promise to make the *issue of dinner* "fun," "super easy to create," "teachable," and "family/couple/group centered." Even if those companies allow their customers to mix and match the recipes, can they truly substitute for personal preferences? I offer my clients the ability to build a personal relationship, discuss what they want to eat, and share how they wish to eat, and I do it all for them. It's the *personal* in being a personal chef that is important to me.

**What would you advise someone who is struggling to build his or her brand?**

Hire a "professional" (someone you pay, even if it's your very reliable cousin-in-law, because people are accountable when they are paid!) to coordinate *all* marketing materials: your website, business cards, flyers, and social media (including utilizing the same user handles for social media). It's easier to brand when you are consistent. If you aren't and you try to improve your branding later like I did, you may end up tied (globally and emotionally) to a moniker or tag line that will become like an old stuffed animal you need to throw out but can't. Additionally, you may need more than one "brand," such as a retail line and culinary instruction.

**Staying motivated when things don't seem to be coming together is a challenge at times. How do you motivate yourself? How would you advise someone else?**

Almost sadly, but probably not uncommonly, what I advise someone else may not be what I do for myself. My advice: you need people, even if you have to pay them. Connect with colleagues and mentors who will listen to your ideas and provide feedback. Socialize with family and friends to disconnect for a bit and recharge. (Sometimes we get caught up in our own heads when we're alone). Again, hire the perfect administrative assistant to push you, remind you of fun upcoming events and past excellent performances, etc. Sometimes, though, "mortgage due" notices are just enough motivation!

**What has been your most effective marketing tool/strategy and why?**

Honestly, my website presence has been my most effective marketing tool. I have very detailed information on my website, and potential and actual clients have shared how much they have appreciated it. Since most people discover my services through internet searches, I use feedback from my website to make use of the tools available to self-boost within those internet searches. My photo and price ranges are on my website very purposefully. I want to help potential clients to be as focused as possible when deciding whether or not to contact me. Everyone's time is precious. Additionally, I am often contacted by potential clients through word-of-mouth referrals from other chefs/caterers, clients, and friends.

**What do you love most about the industry you are in, and how do you stand out in the crowd?**

I love that there is never a dull moment with cooking. Even if I were to teach the same class each week, the participants would be new and the individual results would differ. There's a new party or event every weekend. There's always a new challenge (such as dinner for four in a park without cooking equipment). I may cook for the same group of friends regularly, but each month brings new menus. Also, relationships are built. I can count on my annual Easter brunch family and Thanksgiving drop-offs, and we catch up during those times. I've spent five years with my most senior couple, and I made cupcakes for the husband's 90th birthday.

While I am now paid to cook, *I still do it with love and pure joy*. I keep it personal, and I share the techniques/information with delight. The information is neither a secret nor proprietary. People can truly feel that I want them to learn, and I can impart the knowledge in funny, interesting, and motivating ways.

**One of the biggest struggles entrepreneurs have is how to price themselves. What advice would you share about pricing your services and offerings?**

Be networked and industry-aware. Know what the competition and the profession in general is charging. Know your costs; don't just guess. Yes, price-source ingredients, but also practice cooking with a timer. Do you really know how long it takes *you* to prepare a five-course dinner for eight guests?

Be aware of your abilities, such as self-confidence accented with a touch of humility. Maybe it realistically takes you too long to prepare a five-course dinner for eight guests and still charge your worth; you probably shouldn't offer that service. Or should you charge 50% more than the going rate for pot roast because you really do make "the best pot roast in the world"?

Clearly articulate your pricing and be able to justify it (if only to yourself or closest friend/business partners). Allow wiggle room for potential price adjustments. Know your self-worth and the worth of your assistants. What will be your hourly rate and that of your team members that will be included in your final cost to the client?

**What advice would you give to a chef entrepreneur who is ready to take his or her business to the next level?**

Know your talents and passions as a chef and create other streams of income with those. I love to do cooking demonstrations, and I have found ways to work with that in addition to cooking for my weekly clients. Also, since I focus greatly on a specific diet type, I created a retail line of baked snacks geared for that population. Both of these subdivisions draw attention to my primary personal chef business.

Another crucial tip — hire help! When the clients start coming, you want to be ready to take them all. The help of a part-time administrative assistant and a team of chefs and chef assistants will allow you to become an organized, accessible chef. I have many times obtained clients simply because I was the first one to return their calls with all the answers.

**What "must-have" resources would you recommend someone use in his or her business?**

Staying with my theme, I would say human resources are crucial to running your chef business. I value personal contact because I am an auditory learner and I digest information more effectively when I hear it rather than read it. I do well at workshops and conferences. I am also a tactile learner, meaning I benefit from touching or handling an object. For example, I am energized and motivated through hands-on cooking demos and even through shaking a client's hand.

My must-have human resources:

- Professional associations with regular member meetings, within and outside of your chef career
- Informal team meetings with chefs and chef assistants
- An accountant and/or bookkeeper who can offer pertinent and focused advice on financial management

Because I understand the media world in which we live, I utilize the internet greatly to help me find almost everything. Peruse social media pages of other chefs to see what they are doing. (We post pictures and share articles for this reason!) Use internet searches to find and compare costs for ingredients, chef wear, custom serving dishes, and more. At an interactive cooking party I held, the organizer wanted embroidered chef hats and aprons. I had a very short period of time and a tight budget, and I found a business in Arizona that specialized in exactly what I needed. That business is now a regular vendor, and I recommend them often.

## What makes you a chef who is making an impact?

I know and read about women in their fifties who are showing the world that they are blooming in areas of career, healthy lifestyles, finances, and more. I would like to think that I am part of this group of women.

I am 54 years old, and I recently completely changed careers to pursue what I love. I hope to serve as a positive influence on other women who are considering this type of change. I also hope to show younger chefs that there are options in this field. I have come to understand myself and my own nutritional needs. I am in good health and relatively good shape. As I infuse nutritional health as a part of my cooking, I share with others not only how different foods react in the body, but also that there is no "one diet" for every *body*. I encourage others, especially women, to first understand themselves as they seek solutions to their dietary dilemmas.

The best aspect of my career is providing cooking demonstrations to groups of all ages, but particularly to women over 50. I enjoy swapping cooking stories and sharing tips for healthier eating. My goal is to have a healthy impact and provide an "aha" moment for each participant, one demo at a time.

**What is your favorite part about running your business?**

I can decline a job that I don't want to take, and I can schedule jobs in such a way that I can spend an afternoon at the beach if I want!

**What do you do for work/life balance and to take care of yourself?**

Not enough! But I never have, not even in my first career. The difference now is that I actually know what I like and don't like to do (what makes me feel good or bad), and I am comfortable with those things. I don't have to try out new things. I accept that I enjoy being a couch potato and binge-watching my recorded shows. I love wine and popcorn (my inner Olivia Pope!). I can't wait for periods of time when I don't cook at all for anyone. I love going out to eat and exploring new food places like trendy restaurants, bistros, coffee/tea spots, burger joints, and taco stands. Most of all, I absolutely love a long massage and foot rub!

## Continue the Conversation with Chef Donna Barrow:

 Certified Personal Chef Donna Barrow delighted friends and family with mouthwatering dishes for years and in 2009, she took her cooking to other kitchens to prepare weekly dinners and restaurant-inspired cuisine.

With the goal of healthier eating, this So-Cal native defines her culinary craft as _California Comfort Cuisine_ and adapts for those with special dietary needs. Chef Donna also offers a line of gluten-free and grain-free desserts and snacks.

A former elementary teacher, Chef Donna relishes opportunities to connect to the classroom. An amazing instructor, Chef Donna shares the joy of cooking at prominent cooking schools as well as private homes for personalized cooking lessons for adults and children.

**Website:**
www.yourplateormineinc.om
www.delectablesbydonna.com

# CHEF ELIZABETH BOURGET
## Founder, Gourmet to Go

**Share with us what your business is and why you wanted to start this business.**

I own a personal chef business, Gourmet to Go, which I started in 2002. My desire was to combine my cooking, marketing, and computer skills to create a sustainable business and heal the world one family at a time.

**What was your motivation for becoming a chef and/or starting your own business?**

My motivation for becoming a personal chef was to first and foremost help people improve their health and eating habits, lose or gain weight, fight disease, and spend more quality time at the dinner table. After my divorce, I realized even more how important it is to gather around the table at the end of the day and share a healthy meal.

I was the owner of A Way with Words and Design before I started Gourmet to Go. I like being my own boss, making decisions, and being able to fully utilize my creative abilities. Personal cheffing lends itself to all of these possibilities.

**What have you learned about yourself through running your business?**

I now know how to source the best, healthiest ingredients for myself and my clients. I have learned how to price and time catering jobs that range from 10 people to more than 100. I have learned whether to hire contractors or employees for events. I have learned how capable I am to think on my feet, put out "fires," and calmly keep the flow nice and easy for my clients. I have discovered what jobs not to take and which clients are not a good fit for me. I have found how important it is to know the sources for ingredients and have integrity in all aspects of business. I must stay true to myself and who I am, even if it means I may need to turn away a client.

**What three things do you wish you would have known when you started?**

I wish I would have known how to outsource better, that I needed a website right away, and that I needed to be more selective with choosing networking groups.

**Can you share some early challenges in your business career and how you have learned to overcome them?**

Since I was 40 years old when I started the business, I didn't feel the need to enroll in a culinary program. I did attend the United States Personal Chef Association's four-day intensive program to get an overview of what was involved. It was harder to establish myself as a personal chef at the time since it was a fairly new industry. I designed complicated menus to "wow" my new clients, but my vegetable prepping skills were only "okay." I discovered fairly quickly that I would have to get much faster with prepping and planning to create a manageable work day.

Now I hire culinary students to do all of my prep. I have also hired helpers to shop at the farmer's market for me and to pick up special ingredients. Another helper unloads my equipment and helps me set up my work station.

I also cater small events; I had to figure out how to do these events on my own. It would have been helpful if I had taken a few courses at a local culinary college to help streamline not only the actual food prep and serving but also the pricing.

A big challenge for all personal chefs is educating the public as to what we do for them and how affordable it is to hire a personal chef. Now that there are so many delivery services trying to mimic what a personal chef does, it's becoming even more difficult to get the message across.

**What three characteristics describe what has made you successful and why?**

1. *Confidence!* I can't emphasize this enough. I was already a confident person, and I have a marketing background and a bachelor's degree in computer studies and business. If you don't have customers, you don't have a business. So when I'm catering, no matter what's going on, I always reassure my client that I have everything under control and that it's going to be fantastic! I also believe in myself and don't allow any thoughts to get in the way of my success.

2. Being a creative problem solver. I think on my feet as I go along every day. Sure, I have menus, recipes, tools, etc., but if I look over a recipe and it doesn't quite sound right or I know a better way to do a procedure, I just change it up. I bring extra ingredients so I have options. Basically, I play with food for a living and still love it every day.

3. Having a passion for helping others. I know that I can heal the world one family at a time with the food I source and prepare. This has been a mission in my life for many years; it started when I lost my mother to cancer when I was nine years old. I believe that putting the best possible food in your body will help you fight off disease and/or heal from disease. I follow the Weston A. Price diet called *Nourishing Traditions* to the best of my ability for my clients and myself.

Putting together these three characteristics — confidence, creative problem solving, and a passion for helping others — is what has made me successful in my personal chef career. Add reliability and professionalism, and that's why I'm still growing my business after 14 years.

**How have you defined your voice in your market?**

Most of my clients have found me via my award-winning website. If they take the time to look it over carefully, they can see how much I've accomplished and how careful I am about sourcing my ingredients and preparing food that they will enjoy and, as a bonus, that their bodies will feel good about. I focus on sourcing meat from locally pastured animals and fruits and vegetables from farmers I trust.

**What would you advise someone who is struggling to build his or her brand?**

I suggest hiring a seasoned marketing professional who is familiar with your industry. You can save yourself some time and money by continuing the momentum rather than reinventing the wheel over and over again. I have been mentoring personal chefs for years, and I do my best to prepare them so they can be successful in this industry.

**Staying motivated when things don't seem to be coming together is a challenge at times. How do you motivate yourself? How would you advise someone else?**

In the beginning, it was difficult to keep up the momentum. I worried whether the business would make it, if I would have enough money to pay the bills, and if my body could sustain the physical exertion required to haul my gear several days a week. I believe that basic motivation has to be bigger than money, status, and other common motivations.

For me, it's all about whether or not I'm making a difference in the world. I believe the biggest reward of all is helping another human being, loving what I'm doing, and knowing that the impact I'm making on the planet each day is a good one. I have designed my business to be sustainable and nourishing, and I make sure each dollar I spend is supporting the businesses and people that I believe are doing the best they can for our planet. It's a tall order, and it's accomplished one dollar at a time.

If you don't have a business that follows your core beliefs, I believe you will eventually lack the ability to motivate yourself and others. I advise each and every person to follow what you believe in and stay true to yourself in business and in all other parts of your life.

**What has been your most effective marketing tool/strategy and why?**

I'm not sure I have discovered this key element quite yet. I know my website and newsletters are effective. I'm currently looking into new ways to leverage my abilities and share my responsibilities so that I can focus on marketing. Like so many small business owners, I have been trying to do it all, and so much gets set aside. I am currently working with a business coach to reassess my business and find out how to bring it to the next level.

**What do you love most about the industry you are in, and how do you stand out in the crowd?**

I love the personal chef industry because it opens so many doors to so many different possibilities. Personal chefs are creative, intelligent, business-savvy people that can walk into a new environment every day and take care of all different kinds of people with many different dietary needs. The industry is fairly new, and there are many different ways to do the work that we do — amazing ways to create a work lifestyle that can meet both the client's and the chef's needs.

Sometimes a lack of specific guidelines and regulations opens doors to whole new worlds, and the personal cheffing industry is no exception. Although I don't care for the physical part of my job — carrying my tools to and from my sites — I love becoming a part of a new family every cook date. It's such a unique opportunity. I know I lose business by not working in a commercial kitchen and delivering meals, but in that situation, I would lose other things, such as building deep, long-term relationships with the people that eat my meals almost every day.

I feel that I stand out from the crowd by following my deep beliefs about food. I have spent years sourcing ingredients — from searching for the best strawberries at the local farmer's market to finding out where I can pre-order a Berkshire pig and getting to know the people that are raising that pig. I have been doing farm-to-table sourcing for much longer than it's been in fashion. It just makes sense to source this way. The quality of the food is above and beyond anything I've found in a supermarket.

I also love to combine many ingredients in a dish. I'm known for making quite extravagant soups. I will bring at least 10 extra vegetables to play with whenever I'm creating my soups. I make my own broth so that I can control the amount of salt in the dish and increase the nutrition content of each bite of my food.

**One of the biggest struggles entrepreneurs have is how to price themselves. What advice would you share about pricing your services and offerings?**

Yes, pricing is always a challenge. I only offer one type of service, which makes it easier to price and guarantees I make a minimum per day. I studied other chef's websites from across the country to get a general idea of the pricing for my chef service.

I used to offer an all-inclusive chef service, but that didn't work very well because groceries kept creeping up. I found that I was better off doing the accounting and billing for groceries separately so that I didn't lose money. I also recommend raising fees on a regular basis, especially for new clients, to stay ahead of the marketplace.

**What advice would you give to a chef entrepreneur who is ready to take his or her business to the next level?**

I would consult with a business coach who is familiar with the personal chef industry, such as Deb Cantrell of chefdeb.com. You could also join with a group of other small business owners in different industries to brainstorm ideas for building your respective businesses.

**What "must-have" resources would you recommend someone use in his or her business?**

I rely on my trade organization, the United States Personal Chef Association. Chefs from this industry willingly share a wealth of knowledge with one another.

**What makes you a chef who is making an impact?**

I have cooked for hundreds of people over the past 14 years. I have also successfully transitioned many people back into the kitchen, helping them to prepare meals for their families again. Even though I lose a client when this happens, I know that they are making use of the food knowledge I have shared with them and are making better choices for their health and wellness.

Every time I shop, I make an impact on the farmers I buy from, the stores that stock the items I purchase, and the people that create and sell the products. In addition, I keep my clients from buying processed food, and they don't need to drive to the market as often. I shop for five dinners in one session.

**What is your favorite part about running your business?**

My favorite part about running my business is the control I have over my time. I decide when, where, and how much I will work.

**What do you do for work/life balance and to take care of yourself?**

I work on my schedule in advance, blocking out a few days per week for recovery and/or paperwork. I belong to a workout center that has enough options to enable me to work exercise classes into my schedule several days a week. I get massages and chiropractic adjustments when needed. I get plenty of rest and spread tasks out so that I don't stand for more than six-eight hours per day. I attend my annual conference and go on vacation afterward to make sure I have time to let it all gel.

**Wildcard question! Share whatever you would like the reader to know about you, your business, or your journey. Tell us your story.**

My story started when I was 10 years old. My mother was diagnosed with ovarian cancer and passed away six months later. I watched my father try to heal her through a special diet which included juicing. It didn't work, but it gave me the idea to try to heal people with food.

My maternal grandparents were from Canada and spoke French, and because of this, I was always intrigued with the culture, food, and language of other places. My lifelong dream was to be able to travel to distant lands. My father was a cook in the Navy, so he made some amazing feasts for the holidays. My stepmother's family was Mexican, so they made delicious food during the holidays as well — fresh tamales, baked ham, homemade pumpkin pies, and all the fixings. That's what I remember from my childhood.

After taking a few home economics courses at my high school, I started experimenting with cooking at home. I opened my father's "The Joy of Cooking" cookbook and whipped up a broccoli soufflé and quiche Lorraine. They were fabulous. My stepbrother came out of his room — a rare occurrence — and took some of my food back to his room. He emerged about 10 minutes later and said, "That's the best food I've ever eaten." I figured I was onto something!

I started taking adult cooking classes, scouring cookbooks and markets for unusual ingredients, and learning languages at school. When I was 22 years old, I met my future husband. I made many three- to four-course meals for him. A few years later, we relocated to the Moselle Region in Central Germany.

We spent six years in Germany, and we traveled through Northern Scotland, England, Belgium, Holland, France, many parts of Germany, Spain, Italy, Sicily, Malta, Egypt, Kenya, Luxembourg, and Yugoslavia. I embraced the food, culture, and many times the language of those different places. I took all of the knowledge I gained and applied it to the cuisine I was creating, not knowing that someday I would become a personal chef. Throughout these adventures, I also worked on my bachelor's degree in computer studies and business through the University of Maryland's overseas program.

About five years into our European tour, we started a family. I became a mother of two, who are now 28 and 25 years old. I was the personal chef of my home; I planned, sourced, cooked, and stored food for my family. I was also the owner of a small marketing business called A Way with Words and Design.

Years later, our marriage fell apart. I found myself in a position to reinvent who I was. I found out about the United States Personal Chef Institute, and I signed up for training in Arizona. Upon completion of that training, I jumped right in and started Gourmet to Go. It took a couple of years to make enough for a living, but I persevered because I truly believed this was my calling and that I would eventually be able to support myself and my children.

I had always been a borderline fanatic about the ingredients I purchased, whether or not they were healthy. Unfortunately, a lot of the information I got was from the media — eat low-fat dairy, etc. People asked me to design their menus around so many different diets. Not one of those diets seemed to fit into my concept of healthy food.

Then I discovered the Weston A. Price Foundation. Their cookbook, *Nourishing Traditions*, truly changed my life. All of the recipes are based on research performed by Weston A. Price in the

1930's. He was a dentist who discovered many children with cavities and dental deformities. He decided to travel around the world and search for the healthiest people on earth. He found these people in primitive cultures all over the world. He then decided to study the food they ate and was able to send samples back to the labs in the United States. Years later, Sally Fallon and Dr. Mary Enig put together a cookbook using Dr. Price's food guidelines. I attended a conference that year and found my tribe. Everything they said about food rang true for me. I have been doing my best to follow their guidelines for myself and my clients ever since.

# Continue the Conversation with
# Chef Elizabeth Bourget:

Since 2002, Personal Chef Elizabeth Bourget has been serving families farm to table meals. Chef Elizabeth spent 6 years in the Moselle River region of Germany. She traveled from Northern Scotland to Egypt and Kenyan studying food and culture from each region, working and caring for her family.

After an intensive course at the United States Personal Chef Institute, she launched Gourmet To Go. Although she loves to cook for her families, sometimes she is a "Chef to the Stars". She has prepared meals for Debbie Reynolds, the Canadian Brass Band, Senators and Congresswoman Anna Eshoo and was the personal chef to the CEO of Netflix and his family for 2 1/2 years!

**Website:**
www.gourmetbourget.com

# CHEF GINA VANDERKOOI
## Founder, Higher Seasonings

**Share with us what your business is and why you wanted to start this business.**

My business is Higher Seasonings, and I am a personal chef in Flagstaff, Arizona. I cook locally sourced meals for local families and vacationers in northern Arizona. My love of cooking goes way back, and my path to becoming a personal chef is really a story of two kitchens — the kitchen of my family growing up, and the restaurant kitchens I have worked in all my life.

When I was eight years old, the one book I constantly checked out from the school library was a Disney cookbook, and the first thing I made from it was an "un-birthday" cake from scratch. I was hooked, and I started hanging out with my mom and Grandma in the kitchen from then on. I picked and prepared fresh foods from their gardens and learned to can and preserve everything we picked. In the summers during high school, I earned money picking seasonal fruits and vegetables at a local farm. My family is very close, and through all of our celebrations, I learned how to make our annual, traditional family foods. I also learned that good food shared with family can draw that family closer. Those times with my family are my favorite memories.

Between graduating from high school and starting college, I washed dishes in a Mexican restaurant. I loved where I worked — Araceli (the owner and only cook in the kitchen) taught me even more about traditional family foods. That summer, she taught me to cook her family's recipes, and I learned how hard and rewarding it is to work in the back of a restaurant.

I went to college with dreams of becoming a journalist, but I left school three years later — in debt and no closer to becoming a journalist than when I had started. I went back to working in restaurants, bakeries, and diners to pay my bills and feed myself. There were times when I would go to work at a bakery at 6:00 a.m.

and work until 2:00 p.m., take a nap until 5:30 p.m., go to work at a pizza place until 2:00 a.m., and go home and start it all again.

At some point, I made the decision that I didn't want to live the rest of my life like that, and I went back to school and earned a degree in nutrition and food science. But instead of pursuing those as a career, I married the man of my dreams, followed his job, and started a family. I chose to stay at home to help raise my daughters instead of working outside the home; I will never regret this choice as I watch them grow into strong, smart, compassionate young women. But after 15 years, I used my nutrition background to become a holistic health coach and tried my hand at a few different direct sales companies. Then I decided that I wanted to make money doing something I have always loved to do — cooking. So I applied for a job as a prep chef at a local high-end restaurant, and I went back to a professional kitchen.

**What was your motivation for becoming a chef and/or starting your own business?**

I was finally motivated to become a personal chef by a string of really bad days at a restaurant where I worked. I was overlooked for a promotion and was falsely accused of talking behind the chef's back, then every idea I offered for menu or recipe development was overlooked. For a while, I became every negative thing that I thought I was being accused of — not worthy, not creative enough, not a success in the kitchen because I hadn't gone to culinary school. It dragged me down so much! But I started taking stock of all of my skills and values and decided that I was going to create my own business and be my own boss. What I didn't realize was that there were already people out there doing exactly what I had imagined for myself — working as a personal chef.

**What have you learned about yourself through running your business?**

First of all, I have learned that I am not cut out to run an office.

I love the thought of being absolutely organized, but on my best days, "organized" means that I can mostly identify what is in each of my piles. Because I am a lifelong student, I feel like I should be able to perform every aspect of my own business. But I don't like bookkeeping or invoicing, and I am slowly learning that it is important to delegate those things that don't bring joy or just drain my time and energy. It was initially really hard to let go of that control, but I had to focus on the fact that I was wasting time that I could have been using to find new clients or to be with my family.

I have also learned that I am really good at networking when I put myself out in the community, and that I am good at connecting people with the resources they need. I have always worked hard to develop my listening skills, and I have connected people who are seeking to have a certain problem fixed with those who have the skill and desire to fix those problems. This process also enables me to increase my exposure beyond my local community and reach out to other business owners.

I have also learned that patience is one of the biggest assets for running my own business. Nothing happens as planned on the time line I have set for myself, and feeling under pressure to perform can often lead to a lack of focus.

## What three things do you wish you would have known when you started?

1) It is important to create systems for running your business. Creativity and the ability to create something under pressure or when you are missing key ingredients might be a gift in the kitchen, but it is an absolute detriment when it comes to the day-to-day basics of running a business. I can't count how many times I went to buy groceries and realized I didn't have all of my ingredients on my list, or I started to reconcile my bank statements but couldn't find my receipts. I started my business by doing my own bookkeeping; at the end of the first year, I was three months behind in filing my taxes because I had to find and then enter all of my receipts into my computer. I frequently had

to reprint recipes for one client because I hadn't put them in a binder to take with me. Find a program that can organize your calendar, your recipe file, your idea notebook, and your cooking day — all at once, if possible. I use ModernMeal, and I know there are many other programs available.

2) It's fun to get new ideas from social media and magazines, but be sure to limit the time you spend looking and make sure you are actually creating. I often found myself spending hours on Pinterest or Facebook looking at pretty pictures and fancy platings but never actually writing down my own ideas for dishes or menus. I finally had to delete my bookmarks, donate most of my magazines, and rely on my own instincts to put menus together. I carry a notebook around all the time to jot down any of my inspirations. The ideas may not be relevant to a current project, but when I am later stumped for something original, I will have a great reference of my own ideas to glean from.

3) Be teachable. Go into every new challenge with the mind of a beginner. Find a way to turn any situation into a positive learning experience. The moment you start thinking you know everything is the moment you need to change what you are doing. Every person you meet can teach you something new; every experience is an opportunity to grow stronger.

**How have you defined your voice in your market?**

I provide a special service for people, and I know that I have a lot of ideas and resources that can create healthy, delicious, beautiful meals that busy people often don't have the time to prepare for themselves. When I started my business, I wanted to be able to share every bit of my knowledge with as many people as possible. I tried to tell everyone I met how much they needed me to help them give their families great food. While I worked hard to find those special families to cook for every week, I received calls from people coming to vacation in my town (Flagstaff, Arizona) who needed someone to cook for them for special occasions — weddings, business meetings, family reunions, etc. I worked to fit them into my schedule.

While I was telling them about the fabulous area I live in and how much I love cooking with local, native ingredients, I finally realized that I was developing my own style of service. I offer whole, locally sourced food to families who are looking to spend more time exploring this amazing area with family and friends and less time looking for a place to eat.

**What would you advise someone who is struggling to build his or her brand?**

Remind yourself often of your story. Have you overcome any obstacles in your life that give you a unique insight into what your chosen clientele might need? Will your reason for being in business resonate with other people? Who are you? Where do you come from? What do you love to do? Go back to the answers to these questions every time you struggle between what you want to do and what you think you need to do. When I took the time to evaluate why I wasn't accepting a request for service, I grew closer to realizing what direction I really wanted my business to go in.

**Staying motivated when things don't seem to be coming together is a challenge at times. How do you motivate yourself? How would you advise someone else?**

When negative thoughts creep into my head, I am motivated on a daily basis by looking back on how far I have come on this journey and realizing how much I accomplish each time I move forward. The wisdom that comes from each choice I have made and continue to make can't be taken away. It only grows and makes me stronger. Also, there are people out there whom I haven't met who need my food, and who am I to deny them that?

When I need extra motivation, I listen to personal development gurus. Speakers like Gary Vaynerchuk, Tony Robbins, and Brene Brown really inspire me. They help remind me that my skills will carry me to the next level, that I need to be patient, and that I need to keep working really hard to grow personally and in my business.

Another thing that motivates me is being the mother of two amazing daughters. They have seen how I have turned my crazy ways and ideas into a growing business based around my passion for cooking and serving people. They're smart kids, and I want them to see that patience and hard work pay off. I want to be able to provide them with opportunities to travel around the world while they are still young so they can meet fantastic people and learn from other cultures.

I think the key to staying motivated when things aren't working right — when ideas and clients aren't coming in — is to always remember why you are in business in the first place. Make sure it isn't solely for the money. Continue to grow personally; continue to learn something new every day. Make sure you are always doing something out of your comfort zone. I had to get over my fear of teaching classes by doing a lot of them, and every time I succeed, I realize that the market for teaching is huge and that there are always people who want to learn what I have to teach.

**What has been your most effective marketing tool/strategy and why?**

Networking has been my most effective marketing tool. Don't be afraid of networking, and always keep up with it! Stop handling networking and potential clients as if you are trying to advertise yourself and your services. If you have a passion for what you do (and you absolutely should if you are starting out on your own), you will never feel like you are selling something or being shady. If you light up when you talk about what you are doing, your enthusiasm will be what sells your business. This has become my most effective marketing tool. Get out there and let people know you love what you do. Someday one of the people you have talked to will need your services, or someone they know will need your services, and they will remember your face, not a business card.

**What do you love most about the industry you are in, and how do you stand out in the crowd?**

I was a sociology major at one point in my very long college career. I still love studying people and different cultures, and I love how everyone has a food story to tell. I truly love the rush of preparing many different dishes at once and coordinating them to finish cooking at the same time.

I find it amusing that one of my favorite things about what I do is what keeps people from cooking in the first place — I love to plan menus. I crave the feeling I get when I turn special requests into an amazing menu — revamping a grandparent's recipe or learning a new cuisine that fits a wedding theme. It's like putting together a new puzzle each time, and I get to be the one to choose the pieces that fit perfectly into that puzzle.

What makes me stand out? In each stage of my life, I have been in a situation that most people can relate to. I have grown from a ridiculously poor college student just looking for something marginally nutritious to a successful business person always looking for something new and exciting to eat. I know how hard it is to cook for one person, and I know how hard it is to prepare something that four or more picky people will eat. I can spend hours in the kitchen preparing one special meal, then return later to that same kitchen and, in less than 15 minutes, prepare something to eat on the way to a school event. I can cook a meal based on someone's nutritional needs or cravings, and I can put them all together if necessary. At one point in my search for an amazing career, I felt less than adequate because I didn't have a culinary school background that many of my colleagues had. However, I have all the experience and passion that I need to fulfill many requests.

**One of the biggest struggles entrepreneurs have is how to price themselves. What advice would you share about pricing your services and offerings?**

Research restaurant prices, grocery prices, and delivery service prices in your area to understand what your specific audience is already paying. Never underprice yourself. Account for your skills and previous experiences and value them as resources in the same way that you value your time. Find out if there are other entrepreneurs providing the same services and compare their prices and offerings. Never start too low and expect to be able to easily raise your prices.

**What advice would you give to a chef entrepreneur who is ready to take his or her business to the next level?**

Things began to change for me when I decided to stop being a student. I had to let go of the feeling that I would never know enough to please every client. I recommend that you talk to those people who might be interested in what you do and try to get to the heart of their needs. Determine your key offerings, think about them as separate services, and think about anyone who might need any particular service. How could those people benefit even more from the entire service you offer? Go out and talk to those people right away.

**What is your favorite part about running your business?**

Nothing about cooking for someone else ever gets old. I love making new connections, finding my way around new kitchens, and creating and preparing new recipes. I have always had a tendency to get bored easily when I am doing the same job every day. Not anymore! Every person and every family has a particular dynamic, likes, dislikes, needs, and wants, and I love being able to put all of those pieces together! I am learning to appreciate the power in making my own decisions and learning from the successes and failures that are mine alone.

**What do you do for work life/balance and to take care of yourself?**

I started my own business because I wanted to set my own hours, make my own decisions, and yes, make my own money. However, before I cooked for my first client, I made the decision that my family would always come first; birthdays, vacations, holidays, etc., would be spent with my family. I realize that I am likely walking away from a lot of business when I say "No," but I can't get back the time with my kids and husband. As a personal chef, I give my clients the gift of time to spend with their families, but not at the expense of time spent with mine. When I can, I like to get out and explore new cities and new food with my family and friends. When I can't, I read, hike, and prepare recipes from old Saveur magazines.

## Continue the Conversation with
## Chef Gina Vanderkooi:

 Gina VanderKooi's path to becoming her own boss has been anything but direct. It started when she successfully baked her first cake from scratch at age eight. Since then, she has been a dishwasher, line cook, bartender, graphic designer, food writer, recipe developer, cooking instructor, and holistic health coach. Her personal quest to find a way to connect these interests led her to become a personal chef.

She lives in Flagstaff, AZ with her husband and two daughters, and when she is not cooking with her family, she can be found hiking, designing jewelry, and upcycling vintage clothing.

**Website:**
www.higherseasonings.com

# CHEF JODI GIROUX
## Founder, Jodi's Personal Chef and Culinary Services

**Share with us what your business is and why you wanted to start this business.**

In May 2011, I started Jodi's Personal Chef and Culinary Services in Menomonie, Wisconsin. I offer personal chef services, cooking classes, in-home dinner parties, and basically any special event clients want to have in their homes.

Before opening my business, I worked as a veterinary technician for about nine years. During that time, I also bartended to make ends meet. I worked in small country bars where I had to do it all: bartend, cook, and waitress. I also occasionally grocery shopped for an elderly neighbor, and I often passed along extra food or goodies to neighbors.

In 2002, I decided to go back to school for my business degree, mainly to open more doors for myself in the veterinary field. I attended the University of Wisconsin-Stout (UW-Stout) in Menomonie. All business majors had to take ten credits in another area. The only other thing I knew was cooking, so my "emphasis" became the restaurant and tourism program. This included taking several classes in the restaurant area.

I went to work early and stayed late, but five weeks after school started, the vet clinic let me go due to my school schedule. While I was devastated, my career took a whole new direction. Within a month, I was hired as a part-time cook at Dunn County Health Care Center in Menomonie. We cooked from scratch for close to 200 people, including seven different diets, three different consistencies, and one vegetarian. I had nightmares the first month, but I looked around at the elderly working in that kitchen and thought to myself, "If they can do it, there's no reason I can't."

The world of cooking quantity instead of short order was new to me. Trunnion kettles, buffalo choppers, tray lines, steamers, tilting skillets, and Alto Shaam equipment made up a whole new vocabulary. In addition, I had to start waking up at 3:30 a.m. instead of going to bed at 3:30 a.m.!

I had many significant days, but one in particular stands out. One of the patients at the healthcare center was a vegetarian, and when the menu didn't fit her diet, she chose a slice of cheese, a scoop of cottage cheese, or some other quick protein addition to the non-meat items on the menu. When I returned from vacation a few weeks after starting at the healthcare center, I completely forgot about our vegetarian as I chose one of the quick items to send to her. Her nurse, rightfully so, came down and yelled at me, "She's gotten the same thing for four meals in a row! Can't you give her something different?" I apologized and explained that I had just arrived back from vacation and had forgotten about the woman.

That moment sent me on a mission! From then on, I never gave her a quick item again! I made her meal as close as I could to what the general population was having. I had the manager pick up various Boca products to accommodate her meals. Out of close to 200 people I was cooking for on a daily basis, she became my favorite! I got to be as creative as I wanted to be, and she *loved* it! Her nurse sent me her deepest thanks and always knew when I was working because of her meals! Soon other cooks followed.

As I attended classes and labs, several professors suggested I continue to culinary school, as I "had what it took." To this day, I recall saying to one of my professors, "I think it would be neat to grocery shop and cook for people in their homes." He looked at me and said, "Jodi, that is a personal chef, one of the fastest-growing careers right now!" In 2007, six months after earning my bachelor's in business management with an emphasis in restaurant management, I started culinary school at The Art Institutes International Minnesota in Minneapolis. I graduated in 2009 with the dream of becoming a personal chef.

I worked at various restaurants, and in 2011, I started Jodi's Personal Chef and Culinary Services and joined the USPCA (United States Personal Chef Association). I worked up to two additional jobs, then in 2015, I took the plunge to strictly work on my business.

## What was your motivation for becoming a chef and/or starting your own business?

Another reason I obtained a business degree was to prepare myself in case I wanted to start my own business at some point. When I discovered the personal chef industry, I knew I wanted to follow that path. One motivator was the dislike of the restaurant industry. In my 40+ years of life, I have never worked in an environment that could be so disrespectful, abusive, demeaning, low-paying, and undercutting. This doesn't include the drug scene, which involved both managers and employees, that was present in the majority of restaurants I worked in.

I was glad to exit the restaurant industry on a "high" note. At my final restaurant job, I worked with and for an awesome young manager, and for the most part, the restaurant had a very good vibe. Everyone helped and encouraged each other. I actually enjoyed it and was on the menu for my soups: "Hop Along Jodi's Soups." (I had hurt my left foot and worked with my "boot," and the nickname stuck!) This wasn't the only restaurant that had me make the SOD (Soup of the Day); the first restaurant I worked at in Menomonie also gave me this honor. At the last restaurant, I was offered the position of part owner, but I graciously declined because my calling was to my own business.

## What have you learned about yourself through running your business?

Great question! As organized and dedicated as I was in school, having a business was a completely different ball game! It was difficult trying to grow a business while working two additional jobs. But even when I was blessed to be able to work on my business full time, I struggled with time management and wearing all the hats. I haven't "perfected" it yet, but this is a work in progress, and I am on the "better half" of the journey. I think that is one of the greatest things I've learned. We're all a work in progress. Time doesn't stop. As individuals, families, communities, countries, or nations, we're all evolving. Don't beat yourself up; just keep moving forward and learn. Be humble and honest.

**What three things do you wish you would have known when you started?**

I needed a bigger desk! My corner desk just wasn't big enough! I'd end up working throughout the house, and my office was "everywhere!" I now have an 8' x 2 1/2' table, and my corner desk is with my printer. My mom calls it my command post!

There are a lot of hats to be worn, and it gets overwhelming! I had to plan a specific office day. I chose Monday because the stores aren't re-stocked with fresh produce, and it's very frustrating to try to do personal chef services with subpar produce or no produce at all.

Time management is a related topic. It was easy to think that with more time at home, there was more time to get work done. (This was especially true for me after I dropped the other two jobs.) However, that was not the case. I was used to being on the road and pleasing someone else (a manager). Now it's me, in my home, answering to myself! I like this situation a lot better, but I really had to work to form a system!

**Can you share some early challenges in your business career and how you have learned to overcome them?**

Wow! There are so many! As I mentioned, personal chefs aren't common in my area. There were two personal chefs before me, and both moved on to something else. But the seed was planted in me many years ago, and I firmly believe this is what I am supposed to be doing. Many people have said, "Don't you have to be in the cities for that (meaning Minneapolis/St. Paul)?" If only I could have a dollar for every time I have heard that one!

I actually wrote a research paper on personal chefs in a business writing course at UW-Stout, and I found that there was a need here in Menomonie. However, I knew it would take time — time and patience!

Another difficulty is the task of educating people about what a personal chef is, as well as about the difference between personal chefs, caterers, and private chefs. This is still a challenge that personal chefs face all around the country.

## What three characteristics describe what has made you successful and why?

Honesty is so important — not only in business, but also in personal life. Considering our candidates in this election year, I don't think I need to explain! If you don't know something, admit it. If you messed up and can't salvage your mistake, admit it and *apologize!* Be honest with your peers, clients, and acquaintances, as you would want them to be with you! Always treat others better than you hope they will treat you!

Know your worth! I received a message from someone who was having her 40th birthday party in her home. She wanted appetizers to be served in courses, and she also planned to have wine with those courses. So I encouraged her to do wine pairings with the appetizers, and I came up with a menu and price. She thought the price was high, but I explained that the food was made from scratch, was a result of two full days of prep and serving, and required an additional person to help.

On the first day, my assistant and I arrived, unloaded, and began to cook right away. The host worked out of her home, so she was able to see firsthand all that was involved. Within a few hours, she kept walking around and saying, "I'm so impressed! I'm so impressed!" When we finished the first day, we thoroughly cleaned up and left. The next day, I came back with a different assistant. Again the host said, "I'm just so impressed!" We made her 40th birthday a very memorable one! Before her guests arrived, she said, "Jodi, I was initially concerned about the price, but I want you to know it was all worth it, and I was going to mention it to you yesterday, but I thought I'd wait. If you ever need a reference, please let me know, and I'll be more than happy to give you one! I also plan on hiring you again!" She did — for a kids' cooking class. When I gave her the fee (it was my first kids' cooking class), she told me I didn't charge enough!

I am a good listener, personable, and trustworthy. I think these characteristics are very important for a successful business. People appreciate being *heard*, being *respected*, and knowing they can *trust* you. They appreciate it when you have their best interest at heart!

**How have you defined your voice in your market?**

I have defined my voice by my traits and by being unlimited — offering different things to our area. This is meat-and-potatoes country, and while I can still provide that with a twist, I can comfortably offer other items with different flavors that are equally enjoyable!

**What would you advise someone who is struggling to build his or her brand?**

Ask questions! Seek help! Sometimes we have so much going through our minds that we need someone to help us get a little more focused. Just start doing something!

**Staying motivated when things don't seem to be coming together is a challenge at times. How do you motivate yourself? How would you advise someone else?**

Over the last six years, I have learned to surround myself with people who are encouraging, positive, and supportive. These are people I can count on and trust; most are from the church I started to attend during that time, and some are family members. I also benefit immensely from attending the USPCA conference and collaborating with people in my profession.

When motivation becomes a challenge, all I have to do is pick up the phone, send an e-mail, or grab a beverage with one of these amazing people. I discuss my feelings and struggles openly, and I always walk away feeling better and motivated!

**What has been your most effective marketing tool/strategy and why?**

My most effective form of marketing is when people taste my food! This gives them a chance to see what sets my food apart from that of other chefs in the area. Also, I've been able to use testimonials from clients as references.

**What do you love most about the industry you are in, and how do you stand out in the crowd?**

I love that our industry is always in demand. People need to eat, and there are a plethora of food varieties just waiting to be mingled! My menu is limitless. At this point, I don't have a standard menu because that is what a restaurant or caterer offers. I will eventually have some menu options, but I'll include the option of a personalized menu. I don't like to narrow myself to a handful of items.

**One of the biggest struggles entrepreneurs have is how to price themselves. What advice would you share about pricing your services and offerings?**

Members of the USPCA often raise questions about how to price things. I'm in an area where pricing is conservative, but being a personal chef is a fairly new concept. That doesn't mean I underprice myself, although compared to some personal chefs, I am underpricing myself. However, as my confidence has grown, I have become comfortable with my prices.

Research. When forming a quote, I look up what other places charge for their items. I look at grocery stores, restaurants, and anything I can get my hands or eyes on. My quotes usually come out a little higher. Again, this comes back to knowing your value/self-worth. Personal chefs make things from scratch, which takes time, and you need to charge for that. You also need to charge for your expertise. Finally, since you are a personal chef, your clients know who is preparing and cooking their food. In contrast, customers at other food establishments can only wonder how many people touch their food before they consume it.

No matter the business, pricing is hard. As you get experience and confidence, you'll feel more comfortable with your pricing.

**What advice would you give to a chef entrepreneur who is ready to take his or her business to the next level?**

Seek help and just move forward. At times, I have to remind myself that I didn't learn to walk in an hour or a day. So why do I feel like I have to conquer everything in my business in a day? Be patient but assertive.

**What "must-have" resources would you recommend someone use in his or her business?**

Being a member of a local small business chapter, being a member in a professional organization such as the USPCA, and having a very good support team consisting of family and friends who want to see you succeed. Also, I suggest finding a mentor or mentors. Find one or more people in your profession, people who may excel in business, professionalism, and the like. Find a mentor for every aspect you want to improve.

**What makes you a chef who is making an impact?**

For a little over a year, I was the food coordinator at Hope Gospel Mission in Eau Claire, Wisconsin. It's a place where men and women go to improve their lives in a Christian environment. They may be homeless or in between relationships or jobs without a place to go, or they may have just been released from jail. That was one of the most humbling and interesting jobs I have ever had. I saw men and women at their rock bottom, and I had the opportunity to provide something they looked forward to every day — meals and snacks.

Even since I started my business, I have given to local charities. I donate personal chef services to raise money for fundraisers. Many personal chefs disagree with me on this, but I feel it is important because I can't always make a personal monetary donation to these fundraisers and causes.

## What is your favorite part about running your business?

Being in someone's kitchen is my sanctuary! As soon as I unload groceries and equipment and begin my day, I am at peace! I also enjoy working for myself and not having someone to answer to. Yes, I answer to clients, but I am still my own boss.

## What do you do for work/life balance and to take care of yourself?

The Bible says that we are to have a Sabbath Day, and I try to honor that as much as possible. Before I began attending church regularly, I would work around the clock, work seven days a week, or whatever I needed to do! After hearing a sermon about a Sabbath, I worked toward that; I look forward to that! I have a three-season porch decorated in nautical items; it is my peace room. It's where I read, relax, pray, and spend time with friends and family.

Getting together with loved ones to give and receive encouragement and support has also been very effective. I love to take walks and observe the various colors of green, the corn, the soybeans, the little stream as I cross the small bridge; listen to the birds, tree frogs, and crickets; and sometimes even see deer munching on something or crossing the road. That time spent walking is where I get some exercise, but it also helps me to step away from everything and either solve some problems or plan my day. Knowing what you need to do to recharge, relax, and accomplish things is very important.

**Wildcard question! Share whatever you would like the reader to know about you, your business, or your journey. Tell us your story.**

2011 was a huge growth year for me. On January 1, I was let go from a restaurant after only working there for one month — happy New Year to me! That Sunday I attended church for the first time in many years, and I also began working on my business, which I launched in May. I was baptized in August of that same year.

All of that was five years ago, and I am amazed and humbled about how far I've come personally, professionally, and spiritually! I truly am a new person. I've joined and taught small groups for women who've been abused, and I've also taught a class about setting healthy boundaries. I have found the people that truly want me to succeed, and I have amazing friends and an amazing mom. These changes in my life — including accepting God as my Savior — have helped make me the person I've become. I really don't know where I'd be without the support of the USPCA, family members, and my church family. Actually, I do — I'd be in the same situation I was in five years ago, groveling in little to no growth!

## Continue the Conversation with
## Chef Jodi Giroux:

Chef Jodi Giroux has been cooking in various settings since 1998. She received her Bachelor's in Business Administration with an emphasis in Restaurant Management in 2007 from UW-Stout in Menomonie, WI and her Associate's Degree in Culinary Arts from the Art Institute International, Minneapolis, MN in 2009. She became a member of the United States Personal Chef Association and started Jodi's Personal Chef and Culinary Services in 2010 and services Western WI and Eastern MN. She is also a very active member at Cedarbrook Church in Menomonie, WI.

**Website:**
www. personalchefjodi.com

# CHEF SHIRLEY SCRAFFORD
## Founder, My Chef Shirley

**Share with us what your business is and why you wanted to start this business.**

My Chef Shirley is a personal chef business that specializes in cooking for people with specific dietary needs. It helps people optimize their health by eating more nutritiously while working around any special diet restrictions or modifications.

I started this company about a year after discovering that this type of job existed. At first, I planned a joint venture with a friend of mine. She wanted out of teaching and loved to cook, and I was looking for a job but wanted something outside the usual realm of dietetics. I went to college for dietetics and had worked in that field for most of my adult life, but I wanted something different that still involved nutrition. Combining my field of dietetics and my passion for all things culinary seemed like the perfect option.

**What was your motivation for becoming a chef and/or starting your own business?**

I had done catering, restaurant work, and even cake decorating in between dietetics jobs while I traversed the globe with my husband, who was getting ready to retire from the military. I thought it was the perfect time to start my own business because we would not be moving every couple of years. I also had one child just starting school, another in middle school, and another just starting college, so it was a great opportunity to make some money and have some flexibility so that I could be there for them. I thought I would be able to dictate my own hours and schedule so that my work would not interfere with family time. Because, you know, I wanted it all.

**What have you learned about yourself through running your business?**

The first thing I learned about myself when I started my business was that I needed deadlines, even if I made them up. Otherwise I would put things off until they were forgotten or were simply never done. (For example, when I took my business plan and formally typed it up, the work was done, but it was still on several sheets of notebook paper in a folder for a long while. Once I gave myself a deadline of finalizing it before I did my taxes that year, I completed it.)

I learned that I like to be the boss and be in charge of all parts of the business. It was a little scary at first, and I was not above asking for opinions or advice, but the final decision was mine. The buck stopped with me. I did not miss having someone else make decisions, and I liked the feeling of pride when things went well. It was not so much fun when things were less than perfect, but I sucked it up and learned from my mistakes. It was much better to fix my problems than to have to fix someone else's problems.

That said, once I got to the point where I had people working for me, there were other people's mistakes that I had to correct. I learned that I do not like to be the bearer of bad news (that's probably true for most of us), but I also found that it was easier than I thought. I cared so much about the business and wanted it to stay true to my passion and vision, which was to be sure that customers received the very best service and product. Wanting my business to succeed made it easier to do things that were out of my comfort zone because they were for the betterment of the business. My name is on the business, so it always reflects back to me.

Finally, I learned that some people may not be a good fit for my business. I had husband and wife clients who had completely different tastes. I made dishes that I divided and modified to accommodate their preferences. I also made them completely different dishes. When I came to their house, the refrigerator would be overflowing with store-bought rotisserie chicken, pasta salad, and take-out containers. There was not room for the dishes I was making for them. They wanted low-salt foods, but they complained when I made them that way. My service was just not the right fit for them, and eventually I stopped cooking for them. I did not take it personally, and I learned that sometimes you need to let go of a situation that does not work.

It is difficult when you try your hardest and it does not work out. However, I have become much better at not taking these complications personally. I know I've done my best, and if it doesn't work, those clients need someone else or a different solution.

**What three things do you wish you would have known when you started?**

1. I wish I had known how long it would take to handle all the parts of the business. The time it takes to do an actual cook session is only half the time you spend on it. The rest is recipe search and development, menu development, pantry prep, labels, and grocery shopping. Then you have to add client capture, bookkeeping and paperwork, marketing, continuing education, networking, and employee management. You never really know how much time things will take until you do them repeatedly, and experience is the best teacher. It is too bad that it takes time to gain that experience.

You could hire or find a mentor to give you details about how long certain things should take, but some people are faster at planning and slower at execution, while some take forever to reconcile their books and others fly through that stuff. I realized that it took about twice as much time to do the behind-the-scenes work than I had anticipated. It would have been nice to know that when I started.

2. Before I hired employees, I wish I had known how much time the payroll, employee taxes, and scheduling would take. Once again, you do not know until you do it (and once I get enough money, someone else will be doing it). I still would have done it, but it takes more time than I thought it would, and the expense of training and insuring the employees is higher than I had anticipated.

I also had to consider employee turnover. Both of my chefs quit (for different reasons) in the same month while I was out of the country. That was interesting, and I had to travel back and hire someone quickly so that the new chefs would have some training with the departing chefs before they left. It was not ideal, but it ended up working out — just another curve in the road.

3. The last thing I wish I had known was that it is okay to say "No." In the beginning, I was so focused on getting business that I took jobs that were too far away, adjusted pricing to fit within someone else's budget rather than mine, and let people wait until the last minute to give me their selections or tell me they were going out of town and had to cancel. I did not respect my time and talents enough to stand up for myself. Luckily, that has changed, and I have come to realize that the more I respect myself and let the rules and deadlines be known, the more people respect those same deadlines and me. In addition, there is more than enough business to go around, especially in the D.C. metro area, so if I cannot take on a certain client, another one will show up that is a better fit for me. Each client is not the last client. It is okay to say "No" if that is the correct answer at that time.

**Can you share some early challenges in your business career and how you have learned to overcome them?**

Time management was (and my husband would say still is) a challenge for me. In the beginning, I would spend hours working on a menu and tweaking recipes to get them just right. I like to be very organized, and there was always something to organize, whether it was my spices, pantry items, containers, or files. It seemed there was always something else to do — marketing, bookkeeping, and more.

I decided to actually track all my time and write it down. This helped me see where I was spending too much time, and I scheduled tasks and gave them time blocks so I would stay on track. With the schedule, I feel like I know what I have to do and how long to spend on each task. It makes my life less stressful. If the schedule needs to be adjusted at times, that's okay, and I don't let this cause me stress.

I just like the order that it brings to my day and the fact that I have time for other things, since life is not all about work.

Another challenge early on was the feeling of isolation. I was a one-woman show and often worked in an empty house. I had no one with which to share ideas or gain wisdom. It was a lonely first year. After I had been working for a little while, I joined the United States Personal Chef Association. I would have joined earlier, but I was trying to start this business without spending any of my own money, so I had to save up some money from the business to pay for the membership.

It was money well spent. I was lucky to be in an area with a very active local chapter. Being able to talk with other chefs that were doing what I was doing was great. It validated that I was doing it right while giving me extra tips and tricks of the trade that I had not tried. It gave me a place to ask questions and receive feedback that I knew was trustworthy. It provided the *camaraderie* that I had missed as a one-woman show. It was also a great source of leads for business and provided me a place to refer people that were out of my area.

Joining the local USPCA chapter was one of the best decisions that I made, and it had a huge impact on my business and gave me a sense of community that I had been lacking. It was like having a group mentorship, where I could learn and bounce ideas off chefs that had been doing this work for years. I highly recommend having a mentor or group of chefs or seasoned professionals in your chosen field. They are a tremendous resource to share ideas with and learn from when you are getting started and throughout the life cycle of your business.

The first few months of personal cheffing were a wake-up call in terms of the physically demanding aspect — standing and cooking for hours on end and hauling all of my own cookware and prepping materials to each cook job. I soon discovered that the right footwear was worth its price in gold. As I acclimated to the long periods of standing and learned to walk around and shift my weight, the longer days became a lot easier.

One of the comments I still get when I hire new staff is that they are exhausted when they go home from a job. Some chefs I know take a mat to stand on at a cook job, and they say it helps. I have never resorted to that, but I have noticed that the larger houses with stone and tile flooring are not as foot friendly as those with wood and laminate flooring.

## What three characteristics describe what has made you successful and why?

I like to organize things. I organize everything from my files to my spice drawers (I even alphabetize my spice drawers). I have found this to be extremely beneficial as a personal chef and as a business owner. Order is my friend, and it helps me to keep on track with my clients, inventory, employees, and life in general. I think that when you go into someone's home and your equipment and paperwork are organized and presentable, you display a confidence and professionalism that carries over into your work. In addition, I feel better when things are organized, they are clean and ready to use, and I have a plan for the cook job.

I always make a production schedule for each cook session so that I know exactly what I'm making and in what order, and so that I haven't over-booked the oven or another appliance. This schedule also makes me aware of the time involved in each recipe and helps me estimate what time I will be done. It helps me in the menu planning, as well, because I am keenly aware of the time each recipe takes and which ones work well together to produce a quality product in a reasonable time. Now I organize my chef's schedules and payroll responsibilities, as well as my inventory of cooking equipment and client paperwork. The more business you have, the more organized you need to be, or things can get away from you in a heartbeat.

Secondly, I will work at something until I get it done; I guess that means I am persistent. I will work on a menu or recipe until it is right. Not "almost there" or "okay," but exactly right. This trait is not always my friend when it comes to time management. However, it has made my business produce higher-quality service and products, which means that clients stay with me and return if they have put the service on hold for a certain reason. Being persistent helps when there is a lull in business or things are not progressing the way I want. I will ramp up the client capture process and marketing to get those extra clients that I need to fill my schedule and my chefs' schedules. I would rather be over-booked and turning clients away than wondering how I will fill up another day.

This brings me to the third characteristic that has helped make me successful — being adaptable. While I was growing, I was told early and often to adjust. When things changed or something unexpected happened, my grandmother would say, "Well, we just have to adjust." This became even more important during my years as a military spouse. I "adjusted" to 11 different duty stations and 16 different houses in 26 years. I adjusted to different jobs in those locations, both paid and volunteer, and I helped my children adjust to lots of different schools, teams, activities, and churches. As a business owner, you need to be able to adapt and adjust to the clients and to the changing needs of the segment of the community that you serve.

When I started, I thought I would serve busy dual-income families, and that is exactly what I started doing. But 10 years later, they do not make up the majority of my clients. Many of my clients are now elderly individuals or couples that want to stay in their home but are not comfortable or interested in cooking for themselves anymore. They have health issues and need more than take-out and commercially prepared frozen meals.

I also do much more specialty diet work, especially with cancer patients and children with food allergies. This adjustment was a conscious one, as my nutrition background is what sets me apart from the majority of personal chefs. I have capitalized on that fact and have built my company around offering those specialized diets and restorative meals that not all chefs have the training to offer.

# How have you defined your voice in your market?

My voice in the business of personal cheffing centers on the idea that food is fuel and makes us what we are. Our bodies are totally comprised of what goes into our mouths. There is no better way to improve our health than to improve what we put inside ourselves. Food is fuel and medicine combined, and it can be both delicious and nutritious.

I am active in both dietetics and personal chef groups. This enables me to get my voice to both groups of people, as I am not the norm in either group. As a registered dietitian with a personal chef business, I am in an area that not many dietitians are working in, which sets me apart. As a certified personal chef that is also a dietitian, I am set apart in the personal chef world. This works to my advantage in that I can bring a different perspective to my dealings with each group and educate them about the roles of each other.

I am very interested in the two groups forming a relationship, as having a personal chef would help so many people that are struggling with diet and nutrition-related issues. Also, these chefs would be a great resource for the nutrition practitioners. There are so many ways that the two professions can help each other. Dietitians are becoming more involved in the actual culinary aspect of food. I have taught a class workshop to dietitians on how to give a cooking class so that they can help people learn to cook as well as eat, and to highlight healthier alternatives and products. This is important because people will much more readily eat healthy food because it tastes good than just because it is healthy. Flavor and nutrition must go hand in hand, so chefs and dietitians need to work together and promote a healthier diet.

I have been on several local cooking shows and always do healthy, colorful, and flavorful dishes. I talk about the nutritional benefits of the items I am preparing and make it a part of the message whenever I speak. I do not do promotions that go against my brand or do not promote my brand. I seek out alliances with products and people that have the same ideals and goals as my business.

**What would you advise someone who is struggling to build his or her brand?**

Your brand is what you want your company to be known for. It has to be who you are, what you stand for, how you are perceived, and how you do business. It lets customers know what they can expect from you and how you are different from your competitors. My business name, My Chef Shirley, is about what we do — cheffing — and I put my name there because, when I started, I did not have the foresight to make it less personal. Once I started to expand, I thought about changing the name to something less "Shirley," but I decided that if other brands could be successful with a name (Betty Crocker, Wendy's, Ford, Sears, Aunt Jemima — you get the picture), then I could leave my name in there. Once you have established your brand, you can always add a product line or service that has a different name.

If you are having a hard time defining your brand, think about your target audience. What do you provide to them that makes you special? Are you gourmet or comfort-food oriented? Do you provide more event service or regular meal service? Who are your clients? What qualities do you want to be associated with your company? Is the service you are providing what you *want* to be providing? If not, you need to adjust your focus and work on your marketing and website to better exemplify what it is you are trying to say about yourself, your service, and your company. Someone should be able to look at your website and tell what your focus is. That is the first step in how you define and build your brand.

Once it is defined, go out and make some noise! Network, promote, and communicate! Use your contacts to get the word out to prospective clients. Use social media and emails to talk up your business. Your brand tells people what you do, what makes you special, and how they can benefit from your service. You have to be your own best cheerleader, but do not discount the influence of satisfied customers as great cheerleaders, as well. It is often very productive to offer incentive programs to your current customers for leads or signed-on customers. Happy customers are some of the best advertising!

**Staying motivated when things don't seem to be coming together is a challenge at times. How do you motivate yourself? How would you advise someone else?**

Motivation is a very personalized thing, and my motivation is self-centric in that I want to be a success. I do not usually do something unless I feel I can be successful. This may be simplistic, and it may keep me from doing things that I may be good at but am simply not sure I can do. But I want to succeed, and I need to know what that entails and how I will go about doing it. I plan and think things through before jumping into a project. While failure is always a possibility, it does not mean the end of the road, nor does it mean that you cannot learn from a failure and turn it into a success. Once you learn from a failure, you are probably not going to repeat it.

We all make mistakes, whether it is calculating the food cost of a party, the number of jobs necessary to bring in a certain amount of money, or the time needed to pay off a loan for equipment to take your business to the next level. Just because things are not going "as planned" does not mean it is time to give in. It means it is time to ramp it up or shift gears, look at what is happening, and figure out *why* things are not going as envisioned.

At a certain point in my business, I was not bringing in enough to sustain the staff that I had. Luckily, I was on top of the financial books and could see the shift in profit, and I had to make the hard choice to move one of my employees from full time back to part time. She ended up taking another part-time job, and then another. She went from working for me full time to one day per week. Luckily, as I needed more hours, my other chef was willing to step up and take on more.

Running a business, especially with employees, is a balancing act and needs to be constantly monitored and tweaked. There is no autopilot for business. You need to be able to adapt and adjust in order to move in a different direction if needed. If your car is steering toward a cliff, you turn the other way or put on the brakes. The same is true with your company. You are the driving force and the person driving the train that is your business. With that said, you need to have a goal. Otherwise, how do you know where you are trying to take your business? Having a goal that you are striving to reach can also be a positive motivating factor.

**What has been your most effective marketing tool/strategy and why?**

The most effective marketing tool I have is my website. It is not the most state-of-the-art or beautiful thing in the world, but most of my business comes from it. It has the information someone needs to decide if this is the right type of company for them. I have optimized the search engine so that my website appears when people search. That is important to me. If I were to take this to another level, I would revamp my website right away. It is usually what people see first about a business.

The other effective marketing tool I use is networking — not in the "networking group" so much as with fellow chefs and dietitians. If people looking to refer someone know of you and your qualifications, quality of work, and ethics, they will recommend you. Other chefs recommend me if they cannot take on a client or the client has nutrition-related issues. Dietitians refer clients to me because they know I can help those clients in a way that will help ensure that the person follows his or her diet and eats foods that promote better health. I have connections with both groups. For me, networking is about building the personal and professional connection.

Networking is a two-way process. You need to develop connections to people that can help you and that you can help. It goes both ways. When I receive customers that I can't take or that I feel would be better served by someone else, I turn that business over to other chefs and dietitians. There is enough business for everyone; the key is getting the right business for you and helping those around you succeed, as well. I try to pay it forward whenever I can. It makes for a win-win situation.

**What do you love most about the industry you are in, and how do you stand out in the crowd?**

I came into personal cheffing because of my love for cooking and feeding people. Food is the very essence of comfort to me, and I like to provide that comfort to others. I enjoy the personal interaction, and it's the reason I have resisted the notion of a commercial kitchen. I feel that coming into the home and interacting (most of the time) with the client provides more than just sustenance from the food. It provides the client with a person that cares about him or her, and it's an important part of the relationship that is built between the client and the chef.

I also love teaching (both my parents were teachers), and the cooking classes I get to teach as a personal chef are some of the highlights of the job. As a dietitian, I taught people what to eat, but as a chef/dietitian, I get to teach people how to make something that is great for them and tastes great, too! It's often about giving them the confidence to even try to get into the kitchen and make something. Once they see that it's something they can do, we build on those first techniques and let them stretch their skills even further. This is especially important to do with children and their parents.

This is exactly the reason I volunteered with the "Chefs Move to Schools" initiative that was started by Michelle Obama as part of her "Let's Move" program. Chefs worked with schools to teach cooking skills to students. I ended up working with a school that wanted me to collaborate with parents in an after-school program to teach them to cook. It ended up being a parent and child event, as the children wanted to come too, so we adapted the program to accommodate both. It was a huge success, and we ended up partnering with a second school, as well, teaching after-school cooking classes for middle school children in six-week sessions each quarter. It was also a huge success, and we filled each class.

**One of the biggest struggles entrepreneurs have is how to price themselves. What advice would you share about pricing your services and offerings?**

My first attempt at pricing was very hard. I knew that I wanted to be able to make a certain amount per hour of my time. The problem, as I mentioned before, was that I did not realize how much time it really took. I learned to find out what other personal chefs in the area were charging so I would not be way over or way under the current market price. This helped a lot, and I strongly encourage it. In any business, you need to know your competition, and if your business is similar to those in the market, you need to be able to price yourself somewhere in the market norms.

Your business income needs to cover more than your time and effort. There are more hours put into the job than the hours spent on a client. There is marketing, networking, planning, publicity, bookkeeping, and organizational paperwork, so you need to figure that into the paid hours equation.

Paying for time spent on the job is only one of many business expenses. Make a list of your relatively fixed expenses: organization dues, insurance, business taxes, office equipment (such as a computer, a printer, and supplies), uniforms, cooking equipment, cleaning supplies, a business phone, continuing education, website fees, promotional materials (such as business cards, pamphlets, or car magnets), providers of professional services (such as an accountant, a tax accountant, a lawyer, a photographer, a website designer, a graphic artist, and an agent), a business license, and incorporation fees — and the list goes on. These expenses are business related and are not driven by the number of clients you serve. Other expenses — such as payroll, travel or mileage reimbursement, groceries, and payroll taxes — will rise and fall with your income and client capacity.

You may not have all of the expenses listed above, but you probably have most of them and/or items that are not listed. As you grow, the list will grow, especially if you open a commercial kitchen or hire more employees. You need to keep track of both sets of expenses to accurately assess your company's financial health and make sure that your pricing supports all the expenses you incur.

**What advice would you give to a chef entrepreneur who is ready to take his or her business to the next level?**

If you are going to the next level, create a written plan and go over the numbers if it involves any added expenses. Do not be afraid to see the numbers, in both good and bad scenarios. Be ready to have a "ramp up period," and account for that in your projections. If you know what to expect, you have a way to evaluate your progress. If things are not happening the way you projected, then you should know in time to make any needed adjustments in either your projections or your course of action.

In my case, I was temporarily moving out of the country and wanted to keep the business intact, so I decided to transition one of my part-time chefs to full time. My plan was for her to be my main chef and take over most of my clients while continuing to handle her own. I also expected her to do the menu planning, client contact, new client capture, business promotion, TV appearances, and cooking classes. I still planned to do potential client communications, bookkeeping, invoicing, and payroll.

I was very optimistic, but my projections for income did not take into account that some of my clients would not easily make the transition from me to another chef. We lost one weekly and one biweekly client in the month or two after I transitioned out. That meant that my full-time chef was being paid for a full week of work while only working three to four days per week. I was paying her for one to two days in which no money was coming in. The empty slots did not fill up as quickly as before, and some new clients did not stay on. It was definitely a rough patch.

In this situation, I had not figured out a plan for a worst-case scenario, but luckily I had a written plan of budget projections that I could use to measure my progress. I was able to correct my course by modifying the chef hours to minimize the effect on my bottom line. You must be able to react to the change in income and expenditures, as well as your level of comfort with the temporary changes in income. If you need to have a certain level of income, you need to plan around that. I suggest that you have a cushion to play with so that you can more easily weather the temporary loss of income and the large expenditure or adjustment to your usual business model.

**What "must-have" resources would you recommend someone use in his or her business?**

I've described my "must-have" resources below:

1. QuickBooks has been a great resource that I use for accounting, payroll, and receiving electronic payments from clients. It allows me to set up budgets and compare actual numbers with my projections, thus allowing me to keep a handle on the financial health of my business. Using it for payroll has been easy and a great help, as well, since I can also e-file and e-pay my federal and state payroll taxes. QuickBooks even reminds me when the taxes are due. QuickBooks (or similar accounting software) is a resource I would recommend to anyone running a business, and it is a must-have if you hire employees.

2. The USPCA has been the best resource for me as a personal chef. It is great for anything from recipes, leads for service through Hire-a-Chef.com, and, most importantly, the experience and knowledge of the membership and leadership. My business has benefited immensely from the local chapter membership, where we meet to share ideas and recipes, answer questions, network, learn, and mentor new members. We help each other with larger events and provide a great sounding board for discussing new ideas. This national support has been wonderful in their work to bring the business of personal cheffing to the public. They provide the membership with various company partnerships and resources to help us grow our businesses, from website and publicity to menu planning software, lead generation, insurance, and business support.

They also provide mentorship to new members, which gets them off to a great start. I feel that, without the USPCA, I would not enjoy the success I have today.

**What makes you a chef who is making an impact?**

Affecting people's lives is the immediate impact of my business. It is helping a client get through chemotherapy with nutritious meals that are well tolerated and flavorful in spite of various taste and oral side effects (as well as esophageal and gastrointestinal complications for some clients due to the type of cancer). It is helping young student athletes with multiple food allergies build up their bodies with nutritious foods that they can eat and still fell like a typical teenager. It is helping an elderly couple stay in their home and eat the healthy, flavorful food they enjoy, rather than resorting to take-out or moving into assisted living.

On a broader level, I make an impact by helping to bring together the chef world and dietetics. I am working to collaborate the United States Personal Chef Association with the Academy of Nutrition and Dietetics. On a district and state level, I am constantly educating dietitians about the ways in which their clients or patients can benefit from personal chefs. I coordinated the USPCA's participation as a vendor at the 2016 Virginia annual meeting. I was also able to introduce dietitians across the state to the world of personal chefs, showing how they can help dietitians' patients with diet modification and adherence.

On a community level, our work with youth and parents in two area schools is making an impact as students learn cooking skills and nutrition in our after-school programs, offered though the school district. Feedback from the classes confirms that the students try new food, prepare at home the foods they prepare in class, and have a great propensity to try new foods. This is huge because many people are moving away from home-prepared meals and toward eating out.

I am a huge proponent of eating together as a family around the dinner table. This is a time to share not only a healthy meal, but also stories of the day, plans, dreams, goals, and values. This may sound like nothing but talking, but there are always different things to talk about. A time for face-to-face communication is always important, especially with active children and busy spouses. While the food is often the focus, it is quality time spent with each other and not in front of the television.

With the busy lives of families, these meals around the table are not frequent occurrences. However, if they happen even a few times a week, they can have a profound effect, as long as the table is a place where open conversation is encouraged. (I will now step down from my soapbox.) I cannot make these families talk to each other by providing the food, but I hope these meals make conversation more likely to occur.

**What is your favorite part about running your business?**

I am a people pleaser, so making people happy with food has always been the highlight for me. I love to make healthy and delicious food accessible to people, either though providing the food for them or teaching them how to make it for themselves. My multi-meal services have one type of satisfaction (providing great food on a daily basis), while special events are all about the taste and presentation. Both deliver a great sense of satisfaction.

**What do you do for work/life balance and to take care of yourself?**

Work/life balance is one of the hardest things when your business is growing and you just want/need to do that "one more thing." I was at the point where the business was encroaching on the time I wanted to reserve for my family. I had decided to avoid weekend work in order to have that family time, since my husband was off on the weekends and my high-school-aged kids were occasionally around. This was one way to keep the work from consuming me and to gain some work/life balance.

Later, a time came when I worked days and then evenings on menus, admin work, and answering emails. I tried to get to the gym or schedule walks with friends, but the balance was shifting in the wrong direction. To shift it back, I decided to give up some of my chef work to one of my chefs. That worked. Then I had the opportunity to move to Toronto since my husband was working on a project there, and I decided it was the break I needed from the daily grind. I still did the admin and bookkeeping, much of the menu planning, and some special events and projects, but I did not do the daily cooking. (It was less freeing than I thought, however, as I did say "Yes" to several projects because I was not cooking.)

I also decided it was time to take care of myself, and I hired a personal trainer to give me the support and program to get myself back into better physical shape. It was exactly what I needed! If you take care of yourself, you feel better and have more energy and more clarity of mind to do better work in less time. Exercise takes time, but it gives you an energy boost to make you a more productive person.

Taking a step back from the daily cooking has also greatly increased my creativity boost. I know it is not possible for everyone to take a year or two from the front lines, but even a week away from the daily grind is enough to energize you and give you that fresh feeling when you return to your job. Everyone needs a break to refresh and re-energize. Give yourself the chance to think about something other than the daily work, and maybe even dream about what you want your future to look like, both in business and otherwise. You are more than your job, so don't let your job take over all of you.

**Wildcard question! Share whatever you would like the reader to know about you, your business, or your journey. Tell us your story.**

I have loved food and cooking for as long as I can remember. I think most people (at least in my mind) love food, but even as a child in elementary school, I would check out cookbooks from the library while my friends checked out storybooks. I loved doing history and social studies projects about the food of a culture or country. In high school, I loved science. I never doubted that I would go to college, so I decided that maybe food and nutrition would be a good fit for me.

Of course, growing up, my jobs had to do with food: I worked in the mall's pizza shop, worked as a server, cook, and shift manager for Friendly's, worked with the university food service as special event server, and worked as a cook for a senior center.

I was able to get a spot with the Coordinated Dietetics program at the University of Delaware, and I took my dietetic internship during my last two years of college. I took the registration exam upon graduation, just a few months after I married my husband and moved to the Upper Peninsula of Michigan, where he was stationed at K.I. Sawyer AFB (located in the middle of a state forest, about 20 miles from Marquette). He graduated six months before I did and was a 2nd Lt. in the USAF.

This started a 27-year voyage around the world with the military. During those years, I was able to work in various areas of dietetics and the culinary field. I worked as a health coach and in clinical dietetics in a hospital, outpatient dietetics, elderly feeding centers, public health and WIC, Private Practice, living centers for the elderly and for the mentally retarded, and a wellness center. In the food world, I had a small catering business in Germany, worked as a line cook, had a cake-decorating business, did grocery store demonstrations, and all the while did a lot of large party entertaining and murder mystery dinners (even auctioning some off for charity).

My experiences in places all over the states and the world gave me the ability to adapt and adjust, as well as to broaden my culinary expertise and skills. I learned German cooking from my German landlord's wife, who took me into her kitchen as I tried to write down what she did, since her recipes were not on paper. I learned Korean cooking in Korea, as we fell in love with the freshness and heat of the cuisine. I used to make my own kimchee, but now you can find it in most international grocery stores.

While in England, which is not necessarily known as the culinary capital of the world, I did learn to make some great Guinness stew, summer berry pudding, and scones. The Thai and Indian food in England was amazing, as well, and I found a new love for those cuisines. I also discovered the finely ground spiced sausages called bangers. Now I make my own leaner version of bangers at home using the spice blend I have developed with my own research and experimentation.

While twice living in Europe, we traveled as much as possible, so I have been to many, but not all, of the areas there. There is always room for more travel. Highlights were Rome, Egypt, Germany, London, Disney Paris, Venice, Scotland, Cambridge, and the entire English countryside. Food, as always, was a big part of the experience, and I have recreated various items from our travels.

I grew up in Delaware, and my mother's parents were Pennsylvania farmers who owned a dairy. I owe them a great deal for my love of good, fresh food (each day we ate what they picked that day from the truck garden) and my interest in dietetics. (My aunt, only five years older than myself, was diabetic, and I was always interested in how she balanced her food and insulin). Once in the military, we moved regularly throughout the US. I learned the cuisines of the polish immigrants in the Upper Peninsula of Michigan; Tex Mex in San Antonio; Gulf Coast seafood and Cajun/Creole cuisine in Panama City Beach, Florida; Memphis BBQ in Arkansas; southern cuisine in Georgia; and eastern shore and multiple international cuisines in areas of Virginia and around the D.C. metro area.

Freshness is important to me at home and in business. I love growing my own vegetables and herbs, and I use the herbs in my business. My garden is special to me, as it brings back memories of my grandparents and of my garden at home during my growing-up years. The best part of those summers was the homegrown tomatoes we picked each morning and ate in our sandwiches at lunch.

I owe a salute to my oldest son, who bought me my first website package for Christmas in 2006. This spurred me on to become serious about my business. I had been slowly starting the business, so he bought me the website package while he was home from college, where he studied computer engineering. The gift included his services to build the site, but he went back to school before he could do it, so I was thrust into the world of website building.

It wasn't perfect, but it did the job and got me my first web customers, and I have stayed with the same service all these years, upgrading my package as needed. Once he bought the website, I figured I had to get serious and really get my business going. If he had not done that, I may have procrastinated, and who knows where I would be now. He spurred me on from the "slow start" stage to the "doing" stage. If you are not yet in the doing stage but are still thinking about it, just take the first step! Once you take that first step, it is much easier to keep going. Just do it!

## Continue the Conversation with
## Chef Shirley Scrafford:

Shirley Scrafford is a Certified Personal Chef and a Registered Dietitian, and she has been the president/owner of My Chef Shirley LLC in the D.C. metro area since 2006. She is a graduate of the Culinary Business Academy and the University of Delaware. She has 35+ years of experience in nutrition and culinary positions.

She and her team specialize in helping people with special dietary needs or nutritional requirements. Her chefs and dietitians provide nutrition counseling, cook sessions, cooking lessons, and corporate presentations. She is a corporate member of the United States Personal Chef Association and is active in the local chapter, as well as in various other dietetics and culinary associations.

**Website:**
www.mychefshirley.com

# About the Compiler
# Chef Deb Cantrell

Chef Deb Cantrell is the Executive Chef and Owner of Savor Culinary Services, a personal chef company located in Fort Worth, TX that specializes in culinary medicine and serving those with unique dietary needs.

Deb is also a #1 Amazon Bestselling Author of the book "So You're a Chef Now What?" a sought-after speaker and culinary business coach who helps chefs across the country grow their culinary business and create a life they love.

Chef Deb has spoken and appeared across the country as a keynote and featured speaker at the United States Personal Chef Association, the American Culinary Federation, the Texas Chef Association, the National Association of Women Business Owners and the eWomen Network, to name a few.

She has made TV appearances on stations like CBS and NBC and her health-related articles have been published in several prominent publications like Fort Worth Texas Magazine. Chef Deb has been in the culinary industry for 15 years and has operated five different successful culinary businesses ranging from a catering company to a restaurant. She hopes to help other chefs build the culinary business of their dreams. She offers a variety of culinary business coaching programs with varying degrees of guidance for chefs.

**Website:**
www.chefdeb.com

Made in the USA
Lexington, KY
24 September 2016